Tom & Cindy,

Kind and happy can be found in ... and now yours here on ... where we both have chosen to ...

Lewis Hunt

Psalm 119:105
"Your Word is a lamp..."

God's Choice
A TRUE STORY OF HEARBREAK AND JOY

LEWIS GRANT

authorHOUSE®

AuthorHouse™
1663 Liberty Drive
Bloomington, IN 47403
www.authorhouse.com
Phone: 1-800-839-8640

©*2010 Lewis Grant. All rights reserved.*

No part of this book may be reproduced, stored in a retrieval system, or transmitted by any means without the written permission of the author.

First published by AuthorHouse 2/16/2010

ISBN: 978-1-4490-7812-6 (e)
ISBN: 978-1-4490-7810-2 (sc)
ISBN: 978-1-4490-7811-9 (hc)

Library of Congress Control Number: 2010900787

Printed in the United States of America
Bloomington, Indiana

This book is printed on acid-free paper.

In appreciation: For my father O.O. Grant an inspiring writer, who was driven to write. To my wife Bernis for her help with medical terms and help with words. To a very good friend to our family who spent long tireless hours editing this work.

Foreword

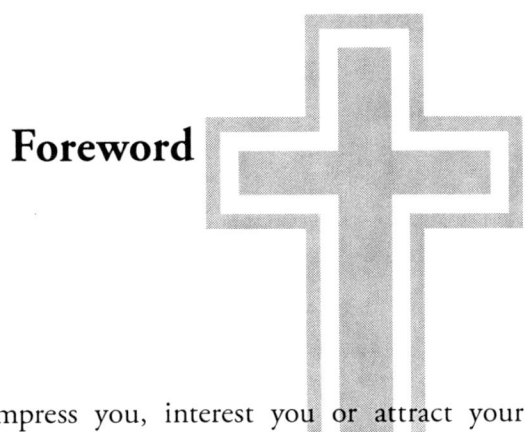

Are there people who impress you, interest you or attract your attention?

This "girl" whose life was lived out in Northern Indiana was not well educated, well spoken or stately in stature, but she did draw attention to herself.

Her professional examiners declared her to have, at best, the mentality of a three year old. She was given every opportunity that a person of her intelligence could handle: speech therapy, sheltered work experience, and training. She was judged teachable but not trainable.

Cheryl was a Down syndrome, mongoloid or mentally and physically challenged person. "Mongoloid" was used to describe her when she was born. Later it was called Down syndrome or just Downs. These days you must be politically correct and say mentally challenged. These are simply different names or terms to describe her condition at different times in her life.

The things about Cheryl that seem to have drawn attention to her are her looks, for sure, but also her personality and the way she interacted with people socially. She loved babies She also loved music, and she didn't hide any of it just because she was in public. If she saw a person who was handicapped in any way such as with a cane or wheel chair, she would take a detour to befriend that person. With normal people she was very selective. Just because you reached out to her did not mean she would let you into her world.

Money never meant anything to her. She ignored dolls, and she could and did entertain herself. Cheryl lived forty-eight years and ten months and died on her absolutely most favorite day of the year, October 31st, Halloween.

So, what kind of experience is it to have a profoundly mentally challenged Down syndrome daughter? It was a wonderful, devastating, heartbreaking, tender learning experience all rolled into this one very real person.

Contents

Foreword vii

Chapter #1 I Have a Life 1

Chapter #2 New Friends/New Home 9

Chapter #3 Logan School 15

Chapter #4 Beverly—Life Changes 23

Chapter #5 Happy Cheryl, Happy Home 29

Chapter #6 Alaska Family 35

Chapter #7 The Beginning of the End 43

Chapter #8 Care Giving Becomes the New Job 51

Chapter #9 Retirement – Not Really 57

Chapter #10 Farewell Bill 63

Chapter #11 A Bad Year 67

Chapter #12 Bad Timing 71

Chapter #13 A Trip to the Ozarks 83

Chapter #14 Too Many Changes 91

Chapter #15 A Long Ending 103

Epilogue **109**

Chapter #1

I Have a Life

"Hey! I have a life, listen to me now. I was born December 15, 1954. My Mom, Beverly Jean Grant, had a huge capacity for love, and she loved ME. She had a hard time carrying me. She even fainted a couple times during my formation, but that had nothing to do with how I came into this world. God decided this place needed me. I guess He figured I could teach my family a few things. Oh, I know you think that extra Chromosome I received made me less, but that is all you know. Do you want to question God? Job did that. Dig out your Bible and look at Job 38, and see what God said to him.

Remember the love I showed to babies? Do you remember how I loved music? Sure, sure, sure, I loved pizza and chicken and pop and 'Donalds, and every other eating place in town, but do you remember, I had compassion too? If you cried, I cried. I would put my hand on your shoulder and ask you what was wrong, and I would comfort you.

I did take a little extra from my parents. Boy, did I burn through the baby sitters. Even I am impressed with 43 years of having them come to sit with me. When I was older my Dad would say to me as he and mom were leaving, 'Take care of So'n So,' and So'n So would earn a few extra bucks because I could take care of myself. I know you will have trouble believing this, but I learned some real good lessons through the years. The experts said my mental capacity was that of a 2-1/2 to 3 year old, but think about this: I would ask for anything I wanted from the kitchen. I was a close observer of what my brother did, whether good or bad, and as he learned, I learned. It may well be that I learned even better than he did. Another thing: I was a safe kid to have in a store or someone's home. I never bothered stuff or destroyed anything. Are you still thinking? Are you still with me? Can you say those things about any so-called normal 2 or 3 year old?

To be sure I had my special friends. Oh, I could be difficult. If I liked you, you were stuck with me, huh? You know who you were, Rachelle, Gino, Patty, Donna Bell, Roberta, Joan, and 'Gib' (Dave), just to name a few. And what if I didn't like you? Forget it! You were not going to change my mind.

So, I hope you have learned your lessons as well as I have. God's gifts come in unusual packages, and sometimes they look like me. Anyway, I am whole now, and I am with my Mom. Just think of me as one of a kind. Come to think of it, that's the way God makes all of us."

Cheryl, or Plum-Plum (Actually I had 'Hey You' write this. 'Hey you', is what I called my dad. I never gave him the satisfaction of calling him Dad, how else could I keep him slightly off balance?)

It was a snowy cold winter day when we brought our firstborn home from Memorial Hospital. We brought her to our home on Grant Street in South Bend, Indiana. It was just a few days before Christmas, and what a great holiday season it would be. This stranger who had been so long in coming would be home.

Beverly had endured so very many days of morning sickness, the whole of the nine months. It had been so severe that she had to be medicated in an attempt to lessen the severity of the incapacitating sessions which became day long instead of just mornings. Beverly had even been the main character in some periods of excitement for those around her. She was the pianist at Twin Branch Bible Church in Mishawaka where we attended. She had continued to play piano part way through the pregnancy. She would even occasionally play the organ. One Sunday morning while she was walking across the front of the auditorium, she unceremoniously fainted dead away!

Such a thing can cause quite a stir. Many, including me, rushed to help her. It was a small congregation, and everyone was understanding and helpful. In that church at that time, everyone knew everyone else, and they all knew Beverly and loved her. They knew of the pregnancy and the problems she was having, and they understood. She was like a friendly little puppy who liked everyone and talked to all who approached her. There would be more excitement to come.

I was a factory worker. The factory where I worked closed down the first week of July every year to take inventory. Employees who were not asked to work or did not wish to work could take that week as vacation. At that time, the company paid its hourly employees a percentage of their previous yearly wage as a vacation bonus. That check provided not only money for our regular bills but was also enough to enable us to take a nice trip as well.

I was born and grew up in a small town in south central Missouri, in the town of Willow Springs. I loved that town, the people, and my relatives who lived in and around the town. The July of Bev's pregnancy we went there to see my folks. In my mother's kitchen was a wood-burning cook stove on which winter or summer the meals were prepared. If you couple that with outside temperatures in the nineties and no air-conditioning, the noon meal in July, at best, was unpleasant. It was one of those days while we were there. We had just finished lunch. Dad saw it first. I heard him say "Oh oh!" as he reached to break Beverly's fall. She had fainted once again. Further along in the pregnancy in our small rented house in Mishawaka, Beverly was washing the evening meal dishes when suddenly she just dropped to the floor! I ran to her and tried to reposition her, but her body was rigid. The skin on her face was drawn tightly across her cheekbones. I was beside myself, terrified with fright! I yelled her name as I grabbed the dishcloth and wiped her face.

She began fighting me, as she came to and pushing my hands away saying, "What are you doing? What have you got in your hand?" I guess the dishcloth did not smell good. Anyway, I was greatly relieved because as she came to it was as if nothing had happened, when I was thinking she must be dead!! That part of our life was over and both of us were thankful, so very thankful.

Beverly named our daughter, Cheryl Catherine Grant. That name went from Cheryl, to Sherry, to Sherry Plum, to Plum-Plum, and that is what stuck, Plum-Plum would be her nickname.

Cheryl's sleeping arrangement would be a little unconventional. At one of Bev's baby showers, she received a car bed. It was about the size of a bassinet. We placed it right beside our bed. When the baby cried during the night, I would jump out of bed, nervous that something was wrong. After a few nights of that, I was a bundle of nerves. I was afraid something would go wrong with that little life God had put in our care.

Beverly had elected to breast feed her new baby, but she couldn't get Cheryl to feed enough to nourish her little body. Cheryl did not seem to have sufficient energy or desire. Breastfeeding just wasn't working.

The doctor we were going to with Cheryl was Doctor Arisman. He was in general practice. Doctor Arisman agreed to take care of our baby for the first year for a one- time payment paid in advance. This allowed us to bring her in or call as many times as necessary, and we were following his directions. When we complained about Cheryl not nursing, our doctor prescribed vitamins in liquid form. He further suggested Bev use a breast pump and feed Cheryl from a bottle. That was working, and the process eventually changed to just formula.

For me to say we knew nothing about babies and how they should act, how they should progress, or much of anything else would be a gross understatement. We just didn't know what to expect. However, we were seeing things that didn't seem right. Aside from the weakness in breastfeeding, the next abnormality was that at one moment as Cheryl looked at us, her eyes looked normal. Then, as she continued to look, her eyes would cross, or one eye would stray and the other would stay focused. She also had problems rolling over. Even as the months moved along, getting her to sit up was out of the question.

We continued to attend church, and no one said anything about the way our baby acted. Beverly was always at the piano, and I led congregational singing. This meant Cheryl had to be in the nursery during the services. Looking back on those times now, it is really hard to believe no one noticed. But then, possibly they were just too kind to say anything. They must have known something was very wrong.

During those days and for many years afterwards Beverly's sister Margie, Bev's only sibling, was a missionary living in Alaska with her husband Roy. They had a baby boy, just a month older than Cheryl. Margie often sent letters to Beverly with pictures and notes, but Bev was not a letter writer, so they did not compare their babies' progress. Also, there was no telephone communication as its cost would have been prohibitive. Because of these things, Beverly and Margie could not help one another through the adventure of motherhood.

When Cheryl reached seven months, and was not sitting up, Bev's mother became very concerned. Yet, she said nothing to us.

Curtis (Shorty) and Elsie McClane, Margie and Beverly's mom and dad, had for sometime been talking about a possible trip to see their new grandchild in Alaska. They decided that the time had come to make that trip.

I remember when we took them to the St. Joseph County Airport and saw them board a DC-6, a four engine aircraft. I also remember that Beverly, Cheryl and I, stood waiting and watching as the pilot labored to get the number four engine to start. Then, through a big cloud of black smoke the engine came to life, and they were on their way.

While Shorty and Elsie were in Alaska at the Lazy Mountain Children's Home where Margie and Roy were serving, mother and daughter were busy comparing notes and babies. They came to the conclusion that Cheryl must have a very serious problem. As strange as it seems now, they did not know what the problem could possibly be. Little did they know that when this drama was lived out in their family, they would recognize a Downs person of any age as soon as they saw that person.

Margie and her mother arrived at a plan. As soon as Elsie and Shorty returned to their home in Indiana, Elsie would insist that Cheryl, now eight months old, be taken to a different doctor, a pediatrician. If she had to stand the cost herself, it must be done.

Why hadn't Bev and I already done this? At this juncture, I can only guess as to why. We were twenty-two years of age, not all that young. We had not had any close contact with other babies. Our friends were younger or a lot older. The younger ones were either just getting married or were married and had had no children yet.

Beverly had been very eager to have a baby. She liked being a mother, and Cheryl was a real joy to her. Bev was using Doctor Spock's book <u>Baby and Child Care</u>. She was happy with Cheryl the way she was. Cheryl was a happy child. She loved being played with or being tossed into the air. The higher she went, the more she liked it. She was tickled at all the attention she received.

Bev and her mother did take Cheryl to see a young doctor who was a pediatrician. That doctor had the bedside manner of a foraging ox. When the doctor asked, "And why did you bring this child to me?" Bev explained that Cheryl was slow, her eyes crossed, and that she could not sit up without help. "We were hoping you could tell us what might be wrong with her," said Bev. The doctor replied, "What is wrong with her? What is wrong with her? She is a mongoloid. Anyone can see that!" The doctor explained what mongolism was and what Bev could expect. He followed that closely by saying, "And you need to put her into a home for such people. There is one here in town near Notre Dame." After such a harsh pronouncement Beverly was in tears, and her heart was breaking.

When I got home from work, Bev was alone with our baby. It was evident that she was very upset as she told me of the trip to the doctor's office. "Cheryl is a Mongoloid," she said. "What is that?" I asked. She handed me doctor Spock's book and said, "Here read this." The edition at that time had a very vivid description of Mongolism: protruding tongue, slanted eyes, thick neck area, plus all the other things that we had noticed. I was crushed, devastated and in tears.

We held each other and tried as best we could to comfort one another. We rehearsed what we had learned, what the doctor had said, and what we had read. As we did, it became clearer what we were up against.

When I got off alone, I remembered having repeatedly prayed and asked God to give us a normal healthy child. It did not matter whether it was a boy or a girl, and now this! I went outside and walked up and down the driveway, crying out to my Lord. "Why? Why, Lord?" It was the most painful thing I had ever faced in my life.

From that day on, every day for the next fifteen years, I prayed that God would heal Cheryl, that He would make her a normal healthy child. I knew that there were differing degrees of retardation, and if it wasn't His will to heal her, I asked that He would make her better or help her in whatever way His will would allow.

After fifteen years, our church had a visiting evangelist speaking. I do not remember what he spoke about or even what his subject was. What I do remember is that I was convicted in my heart concerning my feelings about Cheryl's condition. I finally accepted as from God's hand Cheryl for who she was and as she was. I came to realize that if God had wanted my daughter normal, He would have made her normal when she was born. He is not a cruel God. He would not have put us through all that suffering unless He had a purpose in doing so.

There was a lot of pain and struggle in those fifteen years, actually all forty-eight years and ten months of Cheryl's life. But, I am sorry to say, there was real anger when I began to think of the doctor we had entrusted Cheryl's care to for her first eight months.

Doctor R. K. Arisman was the name of the general practitioner who had the care of Cheryl. As Bev and I went to his office to confront him, it was not a pretty sight. I was very angry. Both Bev and I were broken hearted. The doctor felt guilt free and showed no remorse whatever. His response was: "You loved the child. You seemed happy with her. There was really no help for her. I was doing all that was possible with the medicine I had prescribed. I saw no reason to tell you that your baby was permanently mentally and physically handicapped." Between the tears and the anger, I was beside myself. We never returned to his office.

It seemed such an unfair, unreasonable, total betrayal of our confidence for two doctors to serve us and hide from us the true condition of our child. Doctor George Colip had provided Bev's prenatal care and delivered a Down syndrome child. Yet, he had said nothing about the baby's condition after her birth. Doctor Arisman treated Cheryl for eight months with Bev and me asking, "Why is our child not sitting up? Why can't she roll over? Why are her eyes like they are?" We were left with the fact, like or not, that that was the way they chose to handle it.

Cheryl's next doctor was to see her go through two emergencies. Downs children were all considered to have at least one debilitating weakness in their vital organs. We were soon to learn what Cheryl's was. Her weakness was her respiratory system. She simply could not get over a cold on her own. She always had to have an antibiotic to enable her to recover. If we did not catch it quickly enough, she would begin to have difficulty breathing. And if we did not notice the seriousness of her condition, she would begin gasping for a breath! We would hear this horrible sound, and her little tummy would sink near her backbone as she tried to pull in air. The exercise would be to call the doctor. Then, he would send us to the emergency room with her. They would give her liquid Terramycin, a very thin red liquid that seemed to work the quickest. Next, she would be put into an oxygen tent for a day or two. Then we would continue giving the antibiotic until the cold was clear of her body. The hospital would send her home as soon as she was out of danger.

In 1957 we sold our home in South Bend and started building a new home in Mishawaka. We stored our meager belongings in Bev's folks' garage and moved into their basement. Once again we changed doctors. And once again Cheryl had a severe bronchitis attack. Our new family doctor was C.V. Barone. When we called him and told him what was going on, he prescribed a thick yellow liquid which, when administered, took up whatever space was left for airflow in her throat! We had a desperate situation on our hands. We rushed her to the hospital emergency room. The doctor and I had some very strong words before I was able to convince him that the thin red stuff was what we needed. Our experience told us it was far superior to the thick yellow stuff. Doctor Barone was a "no-nonsense" man. How dare I, a "know nothing," twenty something person, tell him, a medical doctor, how to treat his patient. I was literally fighting for my daughter's life as her doctor stood ready to insert a breathing tube into her trachea.

Thankfully, the doctor relented and changed the medication. After she got the correct medication and was put in the oxygen tent, Cheryl was soon well enough to go back home.

After we learned why Cheryl was not doing all the things expected of her, we settled in with things as they were and began dealing with each problem as we recognized it as a problem. Cheryl did not sit up unassisted until she was eighteen months old. As soon as she was stable enough in the sitting position, we put her in a walker. This contraption had wheels on four long curving legs and was so designed that her feet would touch the floor. With this set-up she could begin to move about the house.

Chapter #2
NEW FRIENDS/NEW HOME

When Cheryl came into our lives, there was more than one change that took place. Some of those changes were in-your-face type things: "Here it is, and you must meet it now." Others were subtler. One dramatic change in a very important area was that of our social life. When it became obvious that Cheryl was different and would continue to be so, we began to have a change-over in personal friends--not all of them, to be sure, but many. People who would invite us over before no longer included us. Time had moved along. They had normal children, and they just stopped including us in their activities. It took some maturing on my part before I could understand what had happened. I now feel they just didn't know how to handle our situation and elected to leave us alone. It did not turn out to be a crippling thing because other people stepped in. People at church watched Cheryl grow. They saw that we were comfortable with her, and they followed our example and became comfortable around her, too.

In nineteen fifty-seven, when we sold our house in South Bend and were living with Beverly's folks, I was busy building a new home for my family. I redesigned the house plans so that there was no access to the basement from inside the house. Anyone wanting to go to the basement would have to go into the attached garage to get to the stairs leading to it. The reason behind this was that neither Bev nor I ever expected Cheryl to be able to navigate stairs. (So much for expected answer to prayer, that God would heal her or at least make her better. I was still praying that He would do exactly that.) I started the new house in

March, and we moved into our home in time to have a New Year's Eve party that year.

The new house had nine hundred square feet of hardwood floors with no throw rugs to get in her way. Cheryl could fairly fly about the house. However, she would not give up the walker and venture out to walk on her own. It took almost another year before she would do that.

It seemed to us that Cheryl would never walk. Her third birthday came and went, and she would not venture out unassisted. But as year number four approached several new horizons were reached. Cheryl had plenty of strength in her legs from the continuous use of the walker, and little by little she started walking. Another thing that had plagued us up until this time was that Cheryl would not, or could not chew her food.

During the time Bev was expecting Cheryl, at a baby shower given for her, she received a beautiful, blond-stained maple high chair. We had been using this chair from the time Cheryl could sit up until the present time. We approached Doctor Barone about Cheryl's refusal to chew. "Doctor, Cheryl loves crackers, cookies, and all kinds of foods, but she won't chew. What can we do?" we asked. "I have no idea. I have never heard of such a thing," he said. We learned to watch her and quickly remove anything that was choking her. We became experts at the finger sweep. Cheryl loved food, and we would keep trying different things in an attempt to get her to chew. It was not a very pretty picture, but we would get her to look at us and exaggerate the chewing motions, hoping she would catch on. Nothing worked. As she neared four years of age it all came together, and miracle of miracles she was chewing.

The fifties was the era of the colored aluminum dishes, and drinking glasses. We had, for a very long time been feeding Cheryl out of one of those bowls, and I had grown weary of having her sweeping it off the high chair tray with a careless move of her arm. Cleaning her, the floor, and all the affected area, was not the most longed for interruption during the family's evening meal. One evening I quietly left the room, went to my toolbox, and removed my drill along with the appropriate size drill bit, a bolt and a nut. I came back to the dining area and drilled a hole down through the bowl and the tray, inserted the bolt and installed the nut. The problem was solved. My wife looked at me, looked down, and shook her head slowly back and forth. Nothing more was said. Living with our Downs child did take some improvising.

Our baby at age four was no longer a baby. She was essentially who she was going to be. It was time for us to accept all that she was and plan her into whatever was ahead for us. We wanted another child. We knew from what our doctor had told us that a Downs child has an extra chromosome, but at that time it was not thought that it was hereditary. All sorts of things were thought to cause this abnormality none of which fit us. Doctor Barone suggested there would be no problem in us having more children.

Being a Christian, in my mind anyway, is a wonderful way to live. However, if you acquaint yourself with the Scriptures, you can't help but find out that there are some things you as a Christian are not supposed to do. Worry is one of those things. But I did worry. I also diligently prayed that our new baby would be normal and healthy. When he was born, he was five weeks early: a premature, five-pound, wrinkled, red baby. When I exclaimed to Doctor Barone how he looked, he said, "He is just premature. He will be fine. He will grow." With that he turned away from me and retreated to whatever his next job was. He had no time for a nervous, anxious father. I don't blame him. I was a real mess. Five years of learning patience with Cheryl's abnormally slow progress had taught us hard lessons as we watched her life unfold.

We named our newborn, Timothy Alan Grant. Compared to Cheryl, Tim's progress was at high speed. Everything happened faster than we expected. We watched in wonder as he progressed. Someone else was watching, too. Very soon Cheryl had a new teacher. Anything in reach was in trouble. Cheryl had never bothered things, but now she would watch her brother do something. Then she would go over and do the same thing.

At the corner of our fireplace we had a planter. The stone came up about twelve inches. On top of that was a tapered copper frame. In this planter was a large split-leaf philodendron that had grown all the way to the ceiling. As it grew it attached itself to the limestone of the island fireplace. Tim would pull leaves off this plant. Cheryl would watch, and pull off leaves as well. Soon the leaves were gone as far up as either child could reach. I would pull the plant loose and stuff the bare stems down and under the copper frame. It wasn't long before our poor plant was completely denuded. When it came to discipline we treated both children the same. That worked fine when they were small. It was a different story as they grew older. The children did learn to leave the plant alone, and it recovered.

In the years that Tim was a baby, we had two baby cribs. Cheryl was not ready to get out of her crib and into a youth bed until about the same time Tim was. As the children graduated to regular beds, a new problem surfaced. Cheryl wouldn't stay in her bed. What I am saying is, she would not sleep in her bed. When we put her down at night, she would go to sleep in her bed. Later, when we checked on her during the night, she would be on the floor. We would put her back into her bed, but in the morning she would be asleep on the floor and not always in her room. Cheryl was never in Tim's room and never in our room. She was usually in the hall, living room, or kitchen. We tried all kinds of things to keep her in bed, but nothing we did was successful. One morning we could not locate her. We were in a panic. Eventually we got down to the basement, and there on top of the ping pong table was Cheryl fast asleep.

Clearly something needed to be done, but what? Over some objections, I decided to remove the lockset from Cheryl's bedroom door and turn it around so the lock could be actuated from the outside. That kept her in her room, but not off the floor. Was the answer to put something on the floor for her to sleep on? No, we tried that, and she avoided that in favor of the bare floor. She always slept on her stomach with her head on her arms, so what was the harm? We gave up until she made the change in favor of the bed.

As I had mentioned earlier, when we built the house, we thought Cheryl would never be able to navigate a stairway or possibly never even walk. I had put the entrance to the basement in the attached garage. Now when Tim was three and Cheryl was seven, the kids were running out through the garage and down the stairs to ride their tricycles. They loved playing together. The recreation room was large and had plenty of room. Their favorite thing to do was to gather as much speed as possible and crash into the paneled wall. This was more than a little hard on the wall, but it was difficult to discourage them, seeing all the glee they expressed at each crash.

The garage basement entry worked all right when it was warm outside, but when cold weather came, the children were catching colds. Since Tim was normal, he could get over a cold without difficulty, but Cheryl was drastically different. It was nothing short of tragic for her to catch a cold. The only thing I could think to do was cut a doorway through the wall into the main entry closet and wall up the garage entrance. Then I put a door in that wall large enough to enable us to take big items in and out of the basement area. It all worked, and one more problem was solved.

Chapter #3
Logan School

Logan school was a facility started for the purpose of helping mentally and physically handicapped children receive as much help as they were capable of absorbing. Beverly was taking Cheryl there every day and picking her up when her classes were over.

Logan was located near the University of Notre Dame. The really great thing about the location was that a lot of the students, either in looking for volunteer work or being assigned that kind of position, made themselves available. When the school had an outing, picnic, camp out, or any activity where individual clients would need help to be there, or in their participation in the event, one of the volunteers would be assigned to them. Through the years, I was privileged to meet some of these fine young people. Our problem was that Cheryl was picky about who she spent time with, and usually she would be uncooperative and a source of frustration for the college student. This, many times, would cause Cheryl's time at these events to be cut short. These times were heartaches for us as well, because it took a lot of effort to prepare things for a non-verbal youth to go camping. Everything that was to go along, including clothes, had to be marked.

It did not take many visits to Logan to realize Bev and I were fortunate that Cheryl's only handicap was that she was a Downs. Many were in wheelchairs, others in specially made chairs where the person was prone or had special fixtures to hold the head. Some made loud noises all the time. Others could not control secretions from their mouths. After a short time there, I was thankful to have our Cheryl as near whole as she was. None of the things I have mentioned ever seemed to bother Cheryl. In fact, quite the opposite was true. All the clients were her friends. Besides that, in public anytime she saw a person with any kind of malady, she would go to them and greet them or pat their arm or back.

Cheryl's life has given me a natural affinity for any Downs I see. I love them on the spot. I cannot help myself. That doesn't mean they return the affection. Nor do I show my affection in any way. Time has taught me that a Downs is not going to warm up to a normal person until they get to know you. There were rare exceptions.

Allison was an exception. Allison lived with her parents just down the street from our home on Terry Lane. She was more advanced than Cheryl. Allison could talk, and she went to school in the special education department in the Mishawaka school system. When I saw Allison in Prickett's Supermarket and she saw me, she would say in a very loud voice, "Mom, Mom, there is Lewie Grant." Her mom would stay in hiding as long as she could. She was embarrassed to have attention drawn to her in public, but nothing embarrassed Allison. She would continue calling her mother until her mother came and spoke to me. Allison was a great friend.

Captiva Island is a great place to be in winter. I was sitting on the public beach there one sunny day. Anyone can go there if they can afford the two dollars per hour to park their car. On the beach that day, an adult Downs was working out. He would shadow box for a while, and then he would practice different types of martial arts. I kept watching him until he went over and sat by an older woman who, I assumed, was his mother. I struck up a conversation with them, during which time I learned that the Downs was a twin with a sister. He was a good verbal communicator. After we had conversed for a while I asked him, "Is your sister like you?" "Naw," he said, "She is just a normal kid." I was impressed at how matter-of-fact he was about how he was compared to his sister.

Another time my wife and I were traveling in Texas. We had stopped in the evening in a rural town to get something to eat. The café matched its surroundings. We found a table. Sitting a few tables away were what appeared to be a father and two Downs boys. The boys seemed to be in their late teens and were dressed in dusty work clothes and boots. All of it fit the backcountry Texas town. The young men's features were much like our daughter's. They were striking. It was not so much their looks though. One of the boys had something in his eye, and he kept rubbing it without having any success. His father was paying no attention at all to his problem. The boy was getting frustrated and was on the verge of anger or tears. I had seen these same actions many times. I wanted to take that boy into the bathroom, and splash water in his eyes until they stopped hurting, something I had done for Cheryl many times. I did not do any such thing. I had a terrible time enduring his suffering while we ate our food. Then I fled the scene.

Things changed considerably over the years that Cheryl attended Logan School, then Logan Workshop, and, finally, Logan Industries. We went through interviews, tours, and more interviews. We entered Cheryl into Logan when she was six years old. There was no transportation available from the school, so Beverly took her in the morning, and picked her up at night. A Volkswagen bug had become the family's number one car. Bev had never driven a stick shift, so I checked her out in it. I got out of the car and, after bridging the negativism, cast her off on her own. She was gone for a considerable time before returning. When she did return, she was ready to use the little car to haul Cheryl back and forth to school. Actually, it became Cheryl and others because other parents were looking for transportation for their child as well.

Beverly was a stay-at-home-mom after Cheryl came to our home, and she did not drive. I had tried to teach her to drive, but I had limited success. Her mother was also giving me a hard time about it. She would say, "Beverly is so short, it will be too hard for her to drive." My response to Mom was, "Aw Mom, Bev's feet touch the ground just like everyone else's. She will be fine". I never was able to teach her to drive well enough to pass a driving test. My younger brother Al was living with us at the time, and he gave her some lessons. In a very short time, she passed her driving test. Brothers-in-law are much more patient than husbands.

At Logan School, Cheryl was evaluated and re-evaluated. She was given speech training, voice lessons, swimming lessons, and more lessons and training than I ever imagined existed. Then every month or so they would have us come in, and they would explain what she had received and what they planned to do next. Oh yes, we were also given her evaluation. This would include what age she was mentally. These things did not discourage us in the least. Cheryl was Cheryl, and at home we were a family. As Cheryl grew, she was given jobs to do. Downs children enjoy working, and Cheryl was no exception to that.

Cheryl was always treated as an equal at our house. She was expected to do what she was told, and when we made it clear what we wanted done, she would give it her best. This would serve her well all of her life. Whether she was in a public place or in a private home, other people's property was safe.

There were times when we were in a store in which fragile merchandise was displayed. We would notice the store clerk keeping an eye on Cheryl. At the checkout counter we were often told that when similar children had been in the store, they had been very destructive. I do not want to paint the wrong picture. Cheryl was not a compliant person. She knew very well what she liked and what she disliked. Cheryl loved all kinds of soft drinks, in her words, "pop." She could bug you to the point where you would begin to believe it sounded like a good idea for Cheryl to have some pop. This is the way she was about any food she especially liked.

I have said that Cheryl was non-verbal. Obviously, that is not true. What happened was that she taught those around her how to communicate with her. One could not sit down with Cheryl and explain a fact to her. She learned by watching others. Living within a family as Cheryl did was perfect for her. She was always watching what was going on, paying attention to what others were doing and listening to what was being said. For example, if I said, "Cheryl, do you want some pop?" With the question, I had gotten her attention. I would not get a direct verbal answer, but soon there was a lip-smacking, smiling, happy person standing very close to me with an expectant look on her face.

One problem we were never able to get around was the difference in meaning between the words "you" and "me." It sounds extremely simple unless you look at it from Cheryl's perspective. If I asked her, "Do you want a cookie, Cheryl?" She got ready to receive the cookie. Fine, but when this was carried over to the family sitting at the table eating, and Cheryl decided she would like more corn, her way was to point to the corn and say, "You?" We would say, "Yes, you may have more corn." If we said, in explanation, No Cheryl, you should say, "May I please have more corn?" Cheryl would be upset and disappointed because, to her, those words meant, I would get more corn and she wouldn't get any. Actually, the way it went was, Cheryl would ask for something (by pointing or by calling it by its name). We would give some to her, or if she had had enough sweets or whatever, we would tell her "no." She would then push the item back away from her. Dessert was Cheryl's favorite part of the meal, so when she had finished hers, she would point, put her finger on the dish holding the dessert and say, "You." We would say, "No Cheryl." She then pushed the dish away with the understanding she could not have any more dessert.

Downs children and adults are known to be loving individuals, and that was true of Cheryl. This trait should not be taken to mean they never get angry or difficult. They are very strong physically as well. When Cheryl reached her middle teens, she was moved to the workshop area of Logan. They also moved the shop area to the old South Bend Toy Works, near the intersection of Lincoln-Way and Chapin Street in South Bend. Parents were still responsible for their child's transportation. For a few months we let Cheryl ride the city bus.

There was another Downs person who lived in the Twin Branch area where we lived. Tom was about the same age as Cheryl, but he was more advanced mentally than our daughter. He had been riding the bus for a while, and he knew when to get off the bus in South Bend where he worked and when to get off the bus when he returned home as well. Cheryl was not able to do these things by herself.

Considering the price of fuel as I write this, four dollars per gallon at my last purchase, I would have been concerned about saving gas money by having Cheryl ride the city bus. It was more about Cheryl getting the experience and the feeling of independence than it was about saving money. One of the goals of the Logan organization was to push the clients out of the nest, so to speak, and the use of public transportation was one more step in that direction.

Beverly still needed to get Cheryl to the bus stop in the morning to meet up with Tom and his father. One of the parents would wait until both of the youngsters boarded the bus. Their return in the evening would occur after I had gotten out of work, so I would pick Cheryl up in the evening at the bus stop.

The care, feeding, development, and responsibility for another human being is never easy, but when you add the Downs equation, the effort not only increases, it also lasts longer. The walk from the bus stop in South Bend to the workshop was between four and five blocks. The winter weather in northern Indiana can be brutal. The conduct of so-called "normal" high school kids can be even worse than the weather because they might poke fun, ridicule, and harass a mentally challenged child. On the one hand, commercial area sidewalks are rarely shoveled in the early morning if ever. On the other hand, Cheryl had cousins who knew what went on in the buses taking kids to Mishawaka High, and it was a bad scene. The bus riding was short lived.

The next thing we tried was taking turns driving, and that worked for a time; however, we were extremely thankful when state money became available for the Logan school and work shop system to have their own buses. Well now, did that solve all our problems? Hardly. Someone had to be home when Cheryl got home. She could not be depended on to use a key to unlock a door, nor would Bev and I be guilt free if something happened to her if the house were left open for her. Anyway, bus drivers would wait until the client was in the dwelling before they would leave. There were times when we had Cheryl dropped off at someone else's home, but that was asking a lot from a driver.

Cheryl would often ride the same bus for a long period of time. Just as often, she would use the same seat, and heaven help the person who sat in her seat, especially if they refused to move when she let them know they were in the wrong place. One evening as Cheryl came in the front door, followed close behind by the bus driver, Cheryl was livid! Angry would not cover it. Her face was covered with blood, but she had no cuts or abrasions. The bus driver was explaining that Harold got into Cheryl's seat before she did and would not give it up. This made Cheryl very upset. "So where did all the blood come from?" I asked. The driver had no explanation. "Harold does not have any injuries either," he said. The blood was on her face and hands but nowhere else. It remained a mystery. I did notice, however, that Cheryl's face was flushed, and for the next several days she had little brown dots where her facial pores were. Did she get so angry that she bled through her pores? I have never heard of such a thing, but I do know that Cheryl could get extremely angry, and if the source of agitation was not removed, things could get out of control. For example, there came a time when Cheryl's punishment had to be verbal only. Even then, if I got after her for something and did not end the thing quickly enough, she would bite her arm. That would take forever to heal because she had exceptionally sensitive skin. It was very susceptible to eczema, and any break in the skin was a big problem.

I do not wish to portray Cheryl as a monster or even as uncontrollable, because she was not. She was, however, an individual with strong feelings. When she reached the age of an adult, she reacted much like any other adult. She knew what she liked and what she disliked, and she had no compunction about letting us know in what category the thing or event fell. It was true, her field of events could be called elementary, but they were monumental to her. The temper flare-ups were few and far between and usually short lived. They usually would involve us complaining about her not doing something good enough, such as washing her hands. She seemed to get bored easily, even with words. We would laboriously teach her a word, and after we had gotten her to where she could say it clearly, she would shorten it to where the only way you would know what she said would be because you had said it so many times you couldn't miss.

I have been writing about Cheryl's undesirable traits, and there was a big one, which was big to us. It seemed to be a necessity for Cheryl, but it was a way she entertained herself. Still, it was a mixed bag. The good part of this bad habit was she used it to fill her time when idle instead of demanding attention from others. Now getting to this big thing: From the time she could do what she wished with her hands, until the time she became so infirm she could not use her hands, Cheryl always used either a toy, a folded piece of paper, a stick or any small item, to tap her face, her shoe or her other hand. If we gave her a stack of papers to write on (make marks on) or draw on, when we left her alone for a time, she would become bored. Then she would carefully fold each sheet into a long narrow fold, tear off the end until it was just the right length, and sit and tap with it.

Another habit Cheryl enjoyed was removing her shoes and picking at the toe of her socks. She would look for a loose thread or seam that was less than perfect, and would work with it until the sock had a hole in it. Then it was back to her sock drawer for a different sock, and the process would be renewed.

Then there were the coloring books and crayons. We tried to get her to color within the lines. She did fine when she was being watched, but when she was left alone, look out. She would make the color sweep the length of the page until the whole page and soon the whole of the book would be a rainbow of color.

I like to think we managed our home in a very normal fashion. At church we took advantage of classes that would teach us how to do that in a good Christian atmosphere with proper discipline, morals, and a spirit of fairness. Part of that meant everyone shared the work. Cheryl was no exception. Her jobs were: close the drapes at night, open them in the morning, and empty the dishwasher. (This occasionally became a problem, if that day Bev decided the dishwasher was not full enough to be run. Cheryl emptied the machine anyway.) Also, Cheryl's job included getting stock from the downstairs pantry. The way we did this was to call Cheryl, show her the item needed (empty container), call out what the item was, tell her to go get it, and hold up the container once again.

Her look would be so very quick it seemed it was not possible for her to really see it. She would immediately go downstairs to the pantry. If the item had been easily accessible, I would have it right away. If it were on a higher shelf, she would pile up books until she could reach it, (leave the books in place), and deliver the item to the kitchen. If the item was not there, I would get something, but she would not come back empty handed.

Chapter #4
BEVERLY—LIFE CHANGES

My dear wife Beverly was a many-faceted treasure of human talent and very good at lots of things. She played the piano with great strength and agility. She was a loving mother and wife. But there was one area where she fell short. That was in the realm of physical agility. In the spring in the early seventy's she was the keynote speaker at Youth for Christ Intercessors at the South Bend YMCA. It was a monthly evening meeting for ladies only. The kids and I busied our selves elsewhere for the evening. It was late in the evening when she finally arrived home. Something was very wrong. Her glasses were broken, and her clothes were somewhat disheveled.

Little by little the events of the evening came out. She told me that the meeting had finished, and she was leaving the new YMCA building. As she descended the steps to the main entrance, she caught her heel in the groove of a tread, lost her balance and fell down the steps. When she fell, she landed on the side of her face and head and was taken to the hospital, treated and released.

Beverly was short of stature: four feet, eleven inches. When she dressed for the evening, she normally wore three-inch heels. Those heel tips fit into the grooves in the step treads. That is what caused the fall. Why she landed on her head is a different problem. In the past, when I saw Beverly fall she never put out her hands to catch herself. The pianist in her would not allow her to do so. She would always protect her hands at any cost.

In the next three weeks several things happened. Beverly began to lose the use of her left side. She was dragging her left leg, and she could not get her left hand and arm to follow her mind on the piano keyboard. She began to have double vision. She had a CAT scan. Nothing showed up. Doctor Barone did a spinal tap to check for blood in the spinal fluid and found none.

It was vacation time, and as usual we had big plans. The Doctor was worried about Bev's condition. He told us in no uncertain terms that he would not allow Bev to leave town. I had made plans to take our boat to Arkansas to fish Norfork Lake and to take Beverly's father Shorty McClane along. Tim, Shorty and I went on the trip while Cheryl and Bev stayed behind. I did not like doing this at all as Bev and I always vacationed together. Besides that, Cheryl loved to travel anywhere. She did not care where we went.

It was three months before Beverly's problems began to clear up. When she told Doctor Barone what was going on, he said, "OK, here is what happened. You struck the right side of your head. The brain swelled on that side and that disabled the left side." We were glad and thankful we could get back to what was a normal life for us as a family.

Things went along fine for five wonderful years. I had gotten promotions at work. Cheryl was doing all right in the workshop. She was even getting paid a small amount for the work she did. Tim was a very healthy boy and doing well in school. Then-- Bev caught a very bad case of the flu. Even before she was totally over the flu, the same disabling of the leg, arm, and the double vision were all back and worse. This time Doctor Barone sent Bev to a neurologist, a specialist.

It was early afternoon when I got the call. Beverly was on the phone, and she was crying. "I want you to come to Doctor Vackors office," she said. She gave me directions. I told my supervisor about the problem and got there as quickly as I could. The Doctor was still with my wife when I arrived. He said, "Mrs. Grant has Multiple Sclerosis," and went on to describe what we could expect from the disease. He then said, "I don't understand what all the crying is about, because when your wife is in her sixties she may need to use a cane to get around, but probably nothing more."

God's Choice

Doctor Vackor had performed a spinal tap on Bev to arrive at his diagnosis. With that information, he was through with us. He sent his findings to Doctor Barone who took over from there. He had us come in and told us what the treatment would be. I was to give Bev injections of Cortisone until the symptoms went away.

It really seemed that our Lord was giving us a hard road to follow, but we were thankful for the good years and good times we had enjoyed, certainly there had been many. We did have our time of weeping, and we did realize after some reading, that Doctor Vackor had given us an overly optimistic outlook for our future.

Beverly was thirty-nine when she fell down the stairs at the YMCA building. It turned out that her age was the only good thing about this whole event. We were advised that the older you are when you get Multiple Sclerosis (MS) the better chance you have of living out your life.

The way it would play out for us was: 1. An attack would come. 2. Medicated or not, it would be with us for three months and then go away. 3. Then, three to five years would go by, and another attack would come. Even though each attack would leave a remnant of the symptoms, Beverly would feel fine in between attacks, and she could carry on her piano playing and teaching. That is the way it went until 1985. Then things changed drastically.

I have used the pronoun "us" when I described enduring this dread disease. Why? Well, when this thing is in your family, you look around to see who else is in the same boat as you are. One of the big things we saw was that when a mate came down with MS, soon afterward there was a divorce! This let us know that this disease must do something to damage the husband/wife relationship, and it does. I was determined that we would see this thing to its ultimate finish.

In the spring of 1972 I made another big change in the use of my spare time. I began taking flying lessons, and in March the following year I received my Private Pilot License. The first thing a pilot has to do after receiving the paper that gives him the privilege of carrying passengers is to take his family for a ride. The plane in which I was certified to fly had only two seats. This meant I could only take one person at a time. When it was Cheryl's turn, she climbed right in. I had learned well in advance of this time that I could not be sure of what to expect of her when we tried something new.

I recall a time on vacation in St. Louis when we decided to take a ride to the top of the Gateway in the West arch. The Arch is located on the waterfront near the heavily traveled bridge crossing the Mississippi river. The little seats used to take us to the viewing area on top wiggled as they moved. This frightened Cheryl, and she could not be comforted. Even when we exited the trolley car at the top, she continued to cry. The government rangers did their best to soothe her, but nothing worked. The place had no peace until we were gone.

Beverly and I both enjoyed the thought of using a private aircraft to do some of our traveling. One of the big attractions was to enable us to fly the six hundred miles to visit my family in south central Missouri, especially the fact that the fence of the home place bordered the airport. To have Cheryl actually enjoy flying was a great boost to our enthusiasm for flying.

Cheryl went flying any time she was asked. I recall one day when we were going to take the *Cessna 150* out to do some touch-and-go landings. The plane sat on a concrete pad and the pea gravel covering the rest of the hanger floor was about three inches lower than the concrete pad. As Cheryl approached the plane, she failed to make the step up from the gravel to the pavement. She stumbled and fell on her hands and knees. This tore holes in her jeans at both knees and removed the skin as well. It also skinned the palm of one hand. She picked herself up, brushed the dirt off her hands, and went "SHOOO" as she pushed the air out of her mouth, took a couple of deep breaths, and that was the end of it. I was amazed at her tolerance for pain. I put bandages on the skinned places, and we went on and had our flight.

Another thing about Cheryl and flying was the noise she would make. She could, and often did, make as much noise as the plane did by making an engine noise with her lips and mouth. Another quirk she exhibited was rocking back and forth when she was idle and enjoying herself. I would notice the plane not staying in trim. When she rocked forward the plane moved with her. When she rocked back, the nose of the plane came up. It was amusing as much as it was a problem, but we had to ask her to stop.

God's Choice

Among the dozens of festivals central Indiana celebrates each year, we chose to go to the Blueberry Festival. It was held near the end of picking season. Those attending were welcomed with lots of food booths and crafts with assortments of unimaginable variety. And there were thousands of people there, looking, buying, and eating their way through the day. We had come to this event to enjoy the day as everyone else had. This is Amish Country. It is not far from Shipshewana the capital of Amish crafts. Much of the food has an Amish flavor as well. It can be enjoyed to the fullest at Das Dutchman Essenhaus in Middlebury. We planned to eat there later that day. I don't remember if anyone else was with our family that day.

It was a perfect mid-summer day, and everything was going as planned until one of us noticed Cheryl was gone. She had started out with us. We were strolling along enjoying everything we saw. Suddenly, she was nowhere to be seen!

From that time until very late in the afternoon, we looked. We asked people if they had seen her, but mostly we just looked. We assumed she was sitting somewhere, but where? We never found her. Instead, she found us. A couple of us were walking along a path, and we heard one of her sounds. (We all have our own.) We looked around, and there she was following us.

There were times during that day when we felt it was hopeless. We thought we would never find her. So when she was found, we did not regret losing a day of enjoyment. Instead, we felt absolute ecstatic elation that she had been found. We couldn't say, "Well, we have learned a lesson, and it will never happen again." It did many times in many different situations, but none were as bad as losing her at the Blueberry Festival.

Chapter #5
HAPPY CHERYL, HAPPY HOME

There was much to be enjoyed having Cheryl living in our home, but we did not keep her to ourselves. She had some very special friends who knew her to be very loving, playful, happy, compassionate and attentive if she liked you.

One of those special friends was her Grandpa Shorty. Beverly's father Shorty was a barber. He was a friend to everyone. He especially liked children, and they liked him. When he was in church and there was room around him. That space filled up with kids of all descriptions. Shorty McClane enjoyed playing with Cheryl. Their favorite game was when he would sing *"Old McDonald Had a Farm"* and let her pick the animal, only he would pick the wrong voice for the animal or Cheryl would. It was hard to tell who laughed the most.

Most of the Downs I saw at the workshop were too heavy. Cheryl was not an exception to that problem. We tried to keep her weight at one hundred eighteen pounds, but Cheryl really loved food and pop. We would give her diet pop, but food intake had to be watched, too. Another problem that entered into the weight control was that Cheryl did not like to walk. I mean she did not care for just going for a walk. I would try anyway. Cheryl was a girl of few words, but oh, did those words have meaning. "Come on Cheryl, let's go for a walk," I would say. Cheryl would respond with, "Oh-boy", (followed by a big sigh) as she removed herself from her comfortable chair and came to follow me.

I first introduced Cheryl to the walking exercise by walking down to the end of our street and back. She so disliked that procedure that any mention of walking put her into a spirit of rebellion. I needed to do something to keep exercise in the realm of enjoyment, and a new plan was devised.

Prickett's Supermarket in the Twin Branch area was where we normally shopped. Cheryl loved going to the store. "Come-on Cheryl, let's go to the store," I would say. She would still say "Oh-boy" and sigh, but she would come along willingly. I would park the car as far away from the entrance as possible, walk in the store, circle the outer isle, and pick out something we could use before taking the long way to the checkout counter.

Cheryl was more than a little adventurous and independent. One day after doing our "supermarket procedure," Cheryl's independent spirit created a very big surprise for an unsuspecting shopper. At the checkout counter Cheryl was bored while she waited on Dad to do his thing. She was looking around at other people and saw a person leaving the store who looked like her Dad. She began following the man. Cheryl knew she was not to cross the driveway without holding on to Dad's arm. Cheryl, not being a gentle soul, ran up to the poor unsuspecting stranger, and unceremoniously rammed her arm through his arm! The poor fellow threw his arm in the air, and jumped to the side. He really was startled half out of his wits. No amount of apologizing or explaining that my daughter mistook him for me helped. He couldn't calm down enough to find any words at all, so Cheryl and I made a quick retreat.

On many occasions we went to the mall as a family. We did not have the habit of going down the aisles holding onto Tim and Cheryl's hands, but we did try to stay together unless we agreed to do otherwise. Cheryl would get tired of walking, and when she did, she would start looking for a place to sit down. Sometimes the seat she would find would be back behind a clerk's counter totally out of our sight! By the time we became conscious of her absence, we may have moved to another section of that area, and then she would be lost to us. She was not lost. She was happy to have a place to rest and would stay there until we found her or she was booted out of the clerk's space. In the meantime, we would be hunting, asking people if they had seen her, even getting the guards involved before she would show up looking for us.

Cheryl knew well how to adjust situations to suit her liking. The trips to the grocery store were a long-range answer to my exercise regimen for her. We always needed things from the store, and Cheryl always needed to be encouraged to walk, but she would modify the walk. My plan was a long walk from the car to the shopping cart. I would take the long way around the store with Cheryl in tow to find what was needed. Her plan was to find a place to sit down as soon as she was inside the store. If I had a long list from Bev, it did not mean a long walk for Cheryl. It meant she could sit while Dad searched for items on the list. I would get the long walk trying to find her when I finished shopping.

All of us have a need to know what is going on that will affect us. The same was true for Cheryl. We could never be sure how much she understood. One day, we decided to explain to her what our plans were. It seemed to work, so we adopted this practice any time we got into the car. It did make a difference, but it did not bring total bliss. Thursday evening became the time set aside for the ladies to get their hair done. Cheryl never enjoyed getting her hair done, but she always liked it when it was done. When she got a permanent, it was a real struggle for the hairdresser. When the ordeal was over, she would show it to everyone, even the cows in the fields as we passed by. "See cow, see", she would say, as she bounced the curls with the palm of her hand.

I have mentioned before Cheryl's tender feelings. Actually, her feelings were multidimensional. She did not have to be the one being addressed to know what the feelings of those around her were. We were on an evening flight from South Bend, Indiana, to my parents' home in Willow Springs, Missouri. I had filed an instrument flight plan because it would be dark when we arrived, but there were low clouds as well. Willow Springs is in a rather remote part of the Ozark Mountains, so our destination (above the clouds) had to be established by using navigational stations that were fifty miles away. This gave a lot of room for error.

When we arrived at what our instruments told us was the Willow Springs airport, I brought the plane down to our landing approach altitude. When I did, all we could see was trees! I did a circle of reference to see if we could find the town. We didn't find a town that I recognized.

It was getting dark. We were low on fuel, and we didn't know where we were. The rules for such a situation is: climb, communicate, and confess, which is what we did. By this time the tension in the airplane was so thick you could cut it with a knife. Part of the time, Beverly would be flying the plane while I searched the charts, as the Controller directed us to an airport which had no lights, thus we couldn't see it. When this happened, my voice and the voice of the Controller both reflected that the flight was lost with no way possible to salvage our situation. Cheryl began to cry. She was very aware we were in trouble. What Bev did next surprised me. She said to Cheryl, "Shut up. Be quiet!" She told me later, "I felt like crying too, but I didn't think it would do any good." The Controller ended up taking us into Springfield's large airport, where we could follow the glide slope in. We had just fumes left in the tanks, but it was enough. Cheryl must have judged that Mom sounded angry so maybe things were not as bad as they seemed. We never heard any more out of her until we landed.

 I think Beverly felt entertained at whatever she did, but most of all, she simply burst with enthusiasm when it came to music. Teaching music was a large part of her life, and I suppose, like most teachers, she had her favorite students. One of her most favored students was Patty Matz. Patty, an advanced student, would play piano duets with Bev. Though the piano room was in the basement and had an acoustic tile ceiling, I could hear their laughter all over the house.

 Cheryl and Patty loved each other and were not bashful about showing it. When they were together, it was endless giggles. Patty, knowing how Cheryl always looked forward to Halloween and her job of greeting the "trick or treaters," would nearly always pay a call. One year Patty was dressed to the hilt and totally unrecognizable. When Cheryl opened the door, three costumed figures came right in and sat on the couch. Cheryl wasn't the only one puzzled. Neither Bev nor I knew who those intruders were. Patty had two friends with her. All were Cheryl's friends. As soon as Patty spoke, the jig was up. Cheryl knew who it was, and from then on it was all hilarity.

 I have mentioned before about how Cheryl loved babies. She would often go to the nursery to see them. If allowed, she would touch the babies and coo at them or touch their faces and say, "Ahhhh." Well, babies attach themselves to others, and some of them attached themselves to Cheryl. When they were two or three years old, she would try to escape from them. After that, though, they would be her friends. One day I saw a little four-year-old girl say to Cheryl, "I love you, Cheryl. Do you love me?" Cheryl said, "No!" It was said very abruptly. The little girl was just crushed and began to cry. I tried to comfort her by telling her that Cheryl didn't mean what she said, but the child would not have any of it. Cheryl was like that. Her response to a question rarely matched what the question required. A lot would depend on who was asking, but mostly, verbiage was a risky way of communicating with her. I have seen a person meeting Cheryl for the first time. Just as clear as you please, Cheryl would say, "Hello." The visitor then would assume this was someone to talk with. Not so, and very soon it was abundantly evident.

Chapter #6
Alaska Family

As things moved along for us as a family, both Tim and Cheryl were in their twenties. Tim had been away to college, and eventually he married. As adults Tim and Cheryl were nowhere close to being buddies. They got along, but that is where it ended. Tim's new wife Sherry was not close to Cheryl either. Sherry had been trained to work with the handicapped and was employed in that area for a time. However, Sherry became a wonderful help to Bev and me as Bev's health continued to deteriorate.

One of the things that precipitated Bev's downward slide was totally unrelated to her MS. She had a problem of calluses on the bottom of her right foot. She decided to go see a local podiatrist. He told her he could go into the side of her foot and trim off the spur on the bottom of the metatarsal bone. He further told her it would be no big thing. It would be done in his office, and he had had lots of experience in performing that procedure with good success. That was the way it was relayed to me. He absolutely destroyed her foot! Never again was she able to walk normally without some sort of protective shoe on that foot. It wasn't long before the toes of that foot began to curl-up. We went to a surgeon whom our doctor recommended. He looked at her foot and made some suggestion as to what could be done. When he learned she had MS, his eyes seemed to gloss-over as if to say, why bother?

It has been said, "We begin life with family, and we end our life with family." Certainly some of Cheryl's best friends, the people who were the most help throughout her life, and the very foundation of support were the Gronnings. Early on in this story, I mentioned Beverly's sister Margie and her husband Roy. When Cheryl was born, they were missionaries in Alaska, and their first child Chris was just a month old. When Chris was in the fifth grade, his mother and father became concerned that the schooling available in the remote village where they were stationed was not adequate for their son's abilities. They asked us if we would be willing to let Chris live with us and attend school in the Mishawaka school system. We were more than happy to have him with us. It would be easy for us because Twin Branch elementary school was only three blocks away.

It seemed like a big adventure to us for Chris to board a Bush plane in his village on the west side of Cook Inlet, fly to Anchorage, change planes in Portland, and fly to O'Hare airport in Chicago where we were to pick him up. However, it was no big thing to him. He had lived on the Yukon and Tanana Rivers and flown in and out of those places and the village he had just left. Nothing seemed to bother him including having to live with us.

By the time school started the following fall, the Gronnings would be living just down the street from us, a few streets east, but in the same neighborhood. Roy was suffering with arthritis, and the cold weather in Alaska had gotten to be too much for his health. The Gronning family numbered seven. Chris and Eric were the boys; Bethel, Rachelle, and Jan were the girls. These girls would grow-up to be Cheryl's primary sitters. They loved her, and she loved them. I would become their mechanic and handyman.

Besides being an ordained minister, Roy Gronning was an architectural draftsman. He was able to find employment at an architectural firm in Warsaw, Indiana. Roy had sought out that firm because its specialty was designing churches. There were a few things wrong with his choice. For one, Warsaw was fifty miles away. For another, the job did not pay very well. To offset these two problems, Roy elected to find a cheap place to stay, and only came home on weekends. That arrangement left Margie with the care of five children. After a few years, they were able to purchase a very old, very large home. The home was located on Lincoln Way East near downtown Mishawaka; it was also close to both the public middle school and high school. The location was perfect for them, not only because of the close proximity to schools, but also because Margie did not drive a car. Roy had taken some vacation time at the time they purchased the house, and he and the family fixed up the place to make it livable. Then they moved in. After that, Margie and the kids were left to shift for themselves.

I do not recall being asked to do a lot of repairs, but I kept seeing an ever-enlarging dark spot on the kitchen ceiling, right below the upstairs bathroom. I asked Margie if I could repair whatever was causing the spot. She gave me permission, and Chris asked if he could help. He turned out to be a great help. Anytime I found time to work on the job, Chris was right there to help. We pulled the upstairs stool, traced the lead soil drainpipe, until we found the crack where the pipe crossed the header for a bearing wall. I collected all the stuff needed to repair the pipe: a large mixture of two-part epoxy and some fiberglass cloth. We mixed it all together and wrapped it around the lead pipe, and waited for it to dry. It held. The leak was repaired. Chris and I put everything back together, put the stool back in place, and repaired the ceiling. The job was complete. The really important thing that had taken place was that Chris and I had bonded to such a degree that after that we were friends--not a small thing to happen between a teenage nephew and his uncle.

Some years later, when Chris was a senior at Franklin College pulling a four-point GPA, he was home for the Christmas break working at a shop in Milford, Indiana. He was trying to make enough money to take advantage of an offer of a free ride to the American University in Washington, D.C., for the second semester. Chris was a political science major, and he considered it a great honor to have this offer. Chris's car was a "hand-me-down" family station wagon that he called "The Great White Hope." All his hopes for that trip to D.C. seemed to be dashed when, on his way home from work one weekend, he was passing a car and the wheels caught in some snowy slush. This sent him into an uncontrollable skid that headed him for a mailbox mounted on an I-beam.

The station wagon was not in as bad a shape as Chris was. He was sure that his transportation to and from Washington, D.C., was gone. He found a phone and gave me a call. I came with a chain, towed him to my house, and surveyed the damage. I told Chris if he could live with the looks of the Great White Hope, then a different radiator and a few well-placed licks with a very large hammer would put him back on the road.

We headed off to search the junkyards for a cheap radiator. We found one, but the owner was a stranger to me (I did spend a lot of time at the area junk yards.) and was very temperamental. I asked him to try the fittings for the transmission cooling lines to see if they were rusted in place. He dropped the radiator onto the dirt floor, and said in an anger-filled voice, "YOU DON'T WANT THIS RADIATOR," as he stomped off.

My employment, at the time, required me to constantly deal with such temperaments. My job also gave me about as much authority as I had in the situation Chris and I faced. None! So Chris and I just stood there and waited saying nothing. Several moments passed before the fellow came back, selected a wrench, and loosened the fittings. We paid for the radiator, took it home and installed it. Before the end of the day, Chris's car was drivable.

I questioned him about how he was doing for the cash he was going to need. Even a friend or an uncle had no right to broach such a subject unless they planned to or were able to do something about the need. In those days I never had any extra money. I really wanted to help this promising young man, so I loaned him my Shell Oil credit card for gas and told him I would pay the bills. Nothing was said about repayment. However, many years later, when Chris was a practicing lawyer and a member of a prosperous law firm in Anchorage, Alaska, he sent me a check for about three or four times as much as I paid out that snowy winter.

After Chris graduated from Franklin Collage with honors, he was given a Marshall Scholarship to Oxford University, where he earned his master's degree. Then he enrolled in the University of Michigan where he received his law degree. Then he returned to Alaska where he passed the bar exam to practice law in Alaska.

When Chris had married and established himself in a law firm in Anchorage, he purchased a new home. After that, he wanted to help his family where it was possible for him to do so. Rachelle, one of Chris' younger sisters, had been struggling with her advanced education. Chris and his wife Denise offered to give Rachelle a place to live, and assured her they could get her into a program where she could finish her degree. This offer had added appeal because Rachelle and Denise were good friends, and the arrangement would give Denise some much-needed company. Chris, as a junior employee in a law firm, was expected to work lots of long hours. His wife then had to spend much of her free time alone.

Beverly dearly loved her nieces and nephews, and since Rachelle was single, she was at our house a lot. She and Cheryl always got along very well, and the love between them was easily seen. When Rachelle told Bev of the opportunity that her brother had offered, the two of them hatched up a plan in which they would fly to Alaska. Rachelle would load all her things into her new Ford Escort. The timing of this was to coincide with my vacation, so I could drive her loaded car up the Alcan highway. Then I could use the unused portion of her roundtrip ticket to return to Indiana.

The whole scheme sounded wonderful to me. I enjoyed the thought of every part of the plan. There were three thousand eight hundred miles of highway, most of which I had never seen. I would take a two-man tent, sleeping bag, air mattress, paraffin stove to cook a breakfast egg, and I would be set to go. I had planned to take the Old and New Testament on tape to keep me company and couple that to a sincere desire to appreciate every tree and stretch of roadway along the route.

It was July, 1985, and vacation time for me. We had helped Tim and Sherry buy a small home located about four blocks from where we lived. Their first child had been born in August of 1984. We asked them to watch Cheryl while we made the trip to Alaska, and they consented. Cheryl would be at work each day, and their one-year-old baby would be a joy to her while she was at her brother's home. With all these things in place, I was at ease with going.

Beverly and Rachelle were on their way. I had put them on the plane the day before and spent the rest of the day fitting my traveling equipment and my duffel bag into what room was left for me in the small two-door sedan. I was determined to make it fit no matter what.

I was so excited about the trip that by three am, I gave up on getting a good night's sleep. I got into the little Ford and headed for the Mishawaka entrance to the toll road. From there I traveled to the west side of Chicago. After that, I wanted roads that I had never been on, so I followed I 80/90 until I 90 hooked up with I 94. I followed that to Jamestown, North Dakota. At Jamestown I picked up Highway 52, which I had planned to take up through Minot, North Dakota and on into Canada.

When I got into Saskatchewan, or possibly even some miles before the border, I kept noticing what looked like a dark mud on the front of cars and pickup trucks. There was not much traffic, so it did not remind me of the mystery, except when I saw an approaching vehicle.

I had spent Saturday night on the outskirts of Minot, North Dakota. By the time I cooked an egg over my paraffin stove (a can of paraffin with a piece of cotton rope as a wick), stowed the tent and sleeping bag, and had driven into Canada, it was nearing time for some ice cream. Eventually, a place came into view that looked open and might even have ice cream. They had just what I wanted, but what greeted me when I looked at the front of the Escort ruined my appetite. The front of the car was covered with the same brown stuff that I had seen on the oncoming traffic: grasshoppers! Thousands of grasshoppers were plastered on and around the grill area. I raised the hood, and every crack and crevice was filled with grasshoppers. I tried to find some screen wire, but it was Sunday, and every possible place was either closed or did not carry what I needed. I cleaned the radiator area and every area that allowed air to enter the engine compartment. Throughout the afternoon I kept stopping to repeat the clean-out operation.

Early Monday morning, I found a hardware store that stocked screen wire that would protect the car's radiator. I could not arrange the screen to totally keep the bugs out, but at least it would let the cooling system do its job.

Another problem I had involved the surface of the roads. In the lower forty-eight states, one can drive for hours and pay little or no attention to the surface of the roads. It is not so in northern Canada. The cold weather does a number on the roads, and even though the highway is marked as a red line on the map, the roads are gravel in summer when they are under repair. What I am trying to say is, you simply have to watch the road and steer around the holes in the road!

I had been told I could count on losing a windshield while driving the six days to Alaska. I had also been advised that when I was on a gravel road and saw a vehicle approaching, I should slow down and move as far to the right as possible. I followed all the rules, but I still received several pits in the windshield of Rachelle's new car.

As I looked at the road maps, I saw the highways going out across the great expanse of Saskatchewan and the cities: Moose Jaw, Saskatoon and Lloydminster. To me it was a once-in-a-lifetime thrill, and I gave it my full attention.

The next event would be in Alberta. I passed through Edmonton, Whitecourt, and Grande Prairie on my way to Dawson Creek, British Columbia. As I looked at what was ahead, I noticed how many rivers there were. Just like anywhere else, a river meant the road goes a long way down and a long way back up with a bridge and a river to view while you are there. The big difference seemed to be that here the engineers did not design roads with dirt moved to fill part of the valley. In this part of the world you get the whole valley. If the hill or mountain is steep, so be it, enjoy.

Dawson Creek is the real jumping-off place where during WW II our Sea Bees built a road that started here and journeyed over a thousand miles across the Yukon Territory and Alaska to supply our troops in and around Fairbanks. I can remember going to the theater with my folks to see the story of this famous highway and all the work and hardship it took to build it. I had wanted to see this place since then, and there it was rolling out before me.

I came to mountain range after mountain range. Wow, what mountains! Some were snowcapped. Some had mirror lakes at their foot. All of it was magnificent to behold.

Every night I was able to locate a park that allowed camping, and one of those nights I chose Laird Hot Springs campground. My stop was earlier than usual. After I got my tent set up, I decided to take a walk out to see what the hot springs looked like. As I was walking across a boardwalk that led to the spring, some people were standing on the walkway. When they saw me coming they held up a hand and a finger across their lips and pointed. Cautiously, I looked to see what they were pointing at. It was a moose and her calf. They were close enough I could see the little beard that dangled from their necks. I made a hasty retreat to my camp to return with my camera.

After viewing the spring, I thought it was a good place to take a swim. My days on the road did not always provide a place to bathe, not that I always searched for such a place. When I had first viewed the pool area there were swimmers, but by the time I went to swim, there was no one around. The water was very warm. I worked my way into it, and after a while I even moved closer to where the water came out of the ground. Closer to the source, the water was much warmer.

When I decided to exit the pool, it seemed difficult to do so. I had climbed down some railroad ties to reach the pool. The ties were stacked in such a manner as to form a half step so that only half of the surface of the tie was available to step on. I struggled up the steps using all the strength I could muster using both my hands and feet. When I got over the top tie, I rolled out on the walkway feeling stupid but thankful I had missed what could have been a very bad ending.

It was a summer northern twilight by the time I headed back down the boardwalk to camp. I saw where the moose and her calf had crossed over the walkway on their way to more pasture. My very warm bath allowed for a good long night's sleep. Then I headed on through the Yukon Territory.

I entered Alaska near the village of Tok. At the Tetlin junction I headed south on Highway One. Also, I finally called Beverly to tell her of my progress and that I would see her the following evening. Then, with a time commitment, I felt a pressure that had not been present during the past seven days. I really did enjoy the thought of seeing my wife, though. I even stopped to pick some colorful poppies that were growing beside the road. That was a mistake! Up to this time during my adventure, I had had no problem with mosquitoes. Beside the road that day in Alaska there were fierce, hungry swarms. I couldn't get into the car without them joining me, so I fought with them for the next fifty miles.

Chapter #7
THE BEGINNING OF THE END

Truly, absence makes the heart grow fonder. I was glad to see Bev, and there were Chris and his wife whom I had not seen in years. Then there was Rachelle whose new car I had driven to Alaska. It had a pitted windshield, and it would take me the better part of a day to extricate all the grasshoppers, well not all of them. Some would be a part of that Ford Escort until it was melted down to make another car.

The happy reunion was short lived. The first evening when Bev and I were alone, she said, "I am experiencing the start of another MS Attack!" This was, at best, very disappointing news. I thought I knew what the worst was. I reasoned that this attack would be like or similar to her earlier bouts with this devastating disease. Three months of whatever it brings, and then life would go back to normal, normal for us anyway. There was no way I could have known then that this was the attack that would never end.

I was used to getting up early, but Chris was up and gone before I came out of the bedroom. He would return around 8:00 in the evening and was then ready to go out to eat and socialize. Chris was bent on showing us a good time. He took us salmon fishing. It was only early August but the Salmon were already starting their return back upstream. Chris liked an area south near Valdez. We fished for most of a day. There were lots of fish, but they were not eating what we were feeding. It was still a good experience.

It seemed it would certainly be a lost opportunity if we did not get out and see some of this beautiful state. Chris was very generous with all he had. Their home was new, and our quarters were very nice. Chris also offered his station wagon and suggested we not leave without seeing the Denali National Park and hopefully also see the mountain. Bev and I planned that trip that also included seeing the city of Fairbanks.

I have been crazy about airplanes for as long as I can remember. To have that craze, Alaska was the place to be. I was a pilot and knew what the rules were, but Alaska is different. We would see an airplane parked in the front yard of a home along a country road. This was a common thing to see. I had wondered where they took off and landed, dah! They used the road of course. The laws in Alaska allow that, but not in the lower forty-eight. Even in Anchorage the sky was full of small aircraft on days when weather permitted. Lots of those planes were seaplanes and would have a short towline trailing.

We headed up Highway #3 in our borrowed car toward Denali. We could see the mountain when we were just outside of Anchorage but not when we were at the foot of this famous weather maker. I asked the shuttle driver what our chances were of seeing the mountain. She said, "Well, I have been making this run every day since mid-May, and I have only seen it five times. We had our answer, only a few were privileged and we were not in that number. Beverly was not feeling well. When we were delivered back to our car, we went on to Fairbanks, checked into a very nice motel, and then headed off to find the hospital emergency room. We sat in the emergency waiting room all evening and until well after midnight before we learned Bev had a bladder infection and received the medication to treat it.

The next morning when I woke up, I got out of the motel so Bev could sleep. Chris had asked if I would have the oil and filter changed in his car somewhere along our route, and this was a good time to have that job done. When I found a service station that could work me in, I struck up a conversation with the owner. I asked him how he liked living here. He responded, "I hate it! I hate the winters. It gets to seventy below zero here. Cars won't start. I drag them inside here, and it is like bringing a huge cake of ice inside with you."

"How long have you lived here?" I asked.

"Twenty years," he said. We both laughed.

When Bev was ready to travel, we took Highway Two to Highway Four, the Richardson Highway that follows the pipeline coming down from Prudhoe Bay. At Glennallen we took Highway One on into Anchorage.

Beverly was a very spunky gal. Even though she had a bladder infection and the trunk of her body was constantly tingling from the onset of the Multiple Sclerosis attack, she did not want to miss anything. We shopped downtown Anchorage and went out to eat once or sometimes twice a day. Our time in Alaska was drawing to a close, and we enjoyed one last fling before we caught our late night flight back to the lower forty-eight.

We had a six-hour layover in Portland, but the thing that really sapped Beverly's strength was the long walk at the Chicago O'Hare airport. Our flight in from the west coast was on a very large aircraft, whereas the flight from Chicago to South Bend, Indiana, was a shuttle. The difference in aircraft size caused us to take the long tunnel walk to our boarding gate for the final leg of our flight. Beverly was really weary by the time we took the final steps into our home. I have replayed this in my mind through the years wondering: if I had not allowed Bev to become so tired, would her MS have gone into remission as it had all the many times before? I will never know for sure.

During the fall months of 1985 drastic changes took place. When she got home from Alaska Beverly started using a cane. Then grab bars were needed to help her make the two steps from the garage into the kitchen. Soon they were needed in the bathroom, too.

As things kept going downhill, more and more imagination had to come into play. Bev needed a walker as her balance became less and less stable. I installed a chain as a barrier across and in front of the bathtub. The tub was directly in front of the stool, and in my mind I could picture Beverly tumbling into it, as she struggled up from the stool.

We had a waterbed with a padded rail along the sides, and I had seen Bev teeter as she tried to exit the bed. My fix for that was two ropes from floor to ceiling, anchored at each end with eyebolts. Those ropes supported a bar between them, just above Bev's head as she sat on the side rail.

By November of that year Beverly was using a wheelchair when we left the house. Her forty-five year career as church pianist came to a close. She had not been able to play publicly for four months, and the way things were looking, she would never play again. When Beverly's Aunty McCall died, she left Bev some money. Bev used that money to purchase a nearly-new professional grand piano (six feet eight inches long). She had only been able to enjoy that piano a little over a year, and as the MS progressed the beautiful instrument appeared to hold no interest for her at all.

Just a couple of months before the Alaska trip, I had purchased Bev a new car that really fit her four-foot eleven-inch stature. She loved it. Beverly had picked the color, and she especially enjoyed the power seat. She only drove it a few times in the fall before giving up driving altogether. As her disease progressed and her body continued to fail, another of her loves had to be passed on to others. That was her love of cooking and baking. For a couple of years, she would wheel herself over to the kitchen entrance, and instruct me on what to prepare and how to put it together. That worked for us for a while. Cheryl helped by setting the table. Then, after a few times of being instructed, she fell into her routine of putting things on the table before the meal and removing things after the meal.

Handicapped people had always been special to Cheryl, so her mother being in a wheelchair or using a walker just prompted her to sympathize with her mother. She would touch her shoulder or hug her and ask if she was ok by saying, "You K, huh?" Cheryl would look so very seriously at to her mother expectant of an answer. During these times Bev was still taking care of Cheryl's special needs: seeing that she was properly dressed, that her teeth were brushed, her sanitary napkin was properly placed, and seeing that Cheryl had a proper bath.

During that period of time, Cheryl's life did not seem to change. She went to the sheltered workshop each day. She was picked up in the morning and dropped off in the evening by Logan's faithful bus service. Cheryl really enjoyed her chores. Once she understood what was expected of her, she gladly did it, except when it came to her hygiene maintenance. She simply had no patience for details, whether for washing or using words that to her didn't seem necessary.

God's Choice

All of our family loved to travel. It never mattered where we went, or how long we would be gone. It was a pleasure to be together. Even our son Tim, as he reached the age where he needed to work at a summer job or was off to college, hated not being included in a planned vacation trip. When Beverly reached the point where she could not negotiate the bathroom stop on her own, a little inventiveness was required. The first try at this was to prepare signs to be used on the door of the ladies room. The sign read: "Handicapped person being assisted, please wait". We would wait until we were sure the room was empty, hang the sign on the door and enter. This met with a measure of success, but not always. One day, after we had hung our sign, Bev was doing her business. I was in the stall with her, and I heard someone enter the room. I said, "Busy, I am helping my wife!" This voice came back, "Sonny, you do what you gotta-do, and I will do what I gotta-do. My son is outside in a big hurry, and I gotta-go." I heard a swift flood in the next stall followed by a door slam, and all was quiet again.

It worked best for us to use the men's restroom. If it was a small restroom, I just locked the door. If it was a large restroom, I would wait until the handicapped stall was empty and then quickly push Bev into it. That worked well for road trips, but airport terminals took a more thoughtful approach. First I would go in and scope out the place. I would check to see if a handicapped slot was open, and more often than not, it wasn't. Some guy would be in there changing every dud he had on, and we had to wait. Also in my survey trip in, I would check to see if there was a way to reach the handicapped stall, other than going by the urinals. If that was not possible, I would tell Beverly, (in a low voice), "Urinals on the right," and keep on trucking.

Travel by air could become a very interesting experience. At least it became that for Beverly and me. Before Bev became totally wheelchair bound, we planned a rather long and complicated trip. I had two half brothers. One lived in the Los Angeles area of California, in Anaheim. The other lived in Grants Pass, Oregon. Not knowing any better, I packed the wheelchair and walker, then, checked it in as luggage. At each destination I would call for a wheelchair and one would be brought to the doorway of the aircraft for our use as we disembarked. The wheelchair came with an attendant who pushed the chair and deposited Beverly either at the luggage claim area or at our next gate. This served us quite well until our return trip. When we landed at the Los Angeles international airport, the person attending the wheelchair deposited Beverly at the wrong shuttle stop. The shuttle that was to take us to the right concourse for us to catch our connecting flight did not stop where we were, and Beverly did not have the strength to walk to where we needed to be. I tried flagging the shuttle down, but that did not work. As time became more critical for us to catch our flight, I walked to the shuttle we needed, boarded it, and explained my problem to the driver, a very large black man. He merely nodded and started driving. He then began cutting through three lanes of traffic, and by the time the front of the bus was at the curb where Beverly was, his bus was blocking all three lanes. He very calmly exited the bus and helped Beverly on and to her seat. We made our flight with only seconds to spare.

Small town airports had very different ways of handling handicapped individuals. When we visited my brother Bill and his wife Millie in Grants Pass, Oregon, our flight landed in Medford. There they loaded a wheelchair onto a pallet and used a motorized forklift, to lift the chair up to the portable stair landing where Beverly was able to take her seat in the chair. Whatever worked seemed to be the order of the day.

After we gained experience and Beverly became more dependent on a wheelchair for any change in location, we learned that all we had to do to travel by air was hang a tag on the wheelchair (The tag was supplied at check-in.) and leave the chair at the doorway of the aircraft, while we busied ourselves getting Beverly into a seat. The wheelchair would reappear at the doorway when we reached our destination. However, we were among the last ones to leave the plane because I would carry Bev from her chair to her seat and then carry her back to her chair when we landed. We usually were seated in first class, or bulkhead seating. This had its perks, in many ways.

We never took Cheryl on a commercial flight, so we never found out how she would handle such an adventure. We could never be sure if she would treat it as "old hat," as she did in the many private aircraft flights she fully enjoyed or if it would frighten her as was so often the case. When Cheryl became upset for whatever reason, the situation had to be changed for her attitude to change. To change things on a commercial flight could be a tall order, and we just never took the chance.

Beverly and Lewis with their new baby, Cheryl.

Cheryl, age 40, dressed to go out.

Beverly, ready to play, and Lewis, to sing, at Jan and Gino's wedding.

Jan and Gino entertaining Cheryl.

Cheryl at the family Christmas celebration, after she had been at the group home for two and one half years.

Chapter #8

CARE GIVING BECOMES THE NEW JOB

Beverly had been losing ground since 1985 when we returned from Alaska, but by the fall of 1990 we needed to find help for her while I was away at work. I had used every other resource that I could dream up. I purchased expensive personal portable radios, one for her and one for me. This worked fine in the evening when I needed to attend a meeting at church or go to the store for something. We had counted on the telephone service at work to make me available for her anytime she needed me. Bev's hands had become almost useless, though, and I could not trust her ability to use the phone any longer.

I found that being a caregiver required special alertness regarding changes in Bev. My wakeup call involving Bev's use of her hands was the loss of her engagement ring. Beverly enjoyed her collection of rings. I took just as much pleasure in giving them to her as she did in receiving them. On our twenty-fifth wedding anniversary, I gave her a very nice engagement ring to replace the one I had given her twenty-five years before. That first ring had cost about the same amount as a set of tires for my car. She helped pick out the ring, and we put it on lay-away. When I went back home to see my parents during the July vacation break, I purchased a new set of tires with the money I had set aside to get the ring out of lay-away. That caused a bit of a problem at the time. Now that she was sick, Bev kept her rings in a ring box next to her chair. Each night, just before I got her ready for bed, she removed her rings and stored them in the box until morning. One evening when I came to get her ready for bed, I found one of her rings lying in the middle of the floor. I noticed she had already removed her engagement ring, but it was not in the ring box! I searched around her chair and then all over the room. Nothing! Earlier that night I had emptied her wastebasket and bagged it together with all the other trash in the house. I retrieved the bag of trash and went through it carefully even to the extent of squeezing foodstuff to see if it contained the missing ring. Again, I found nothing.

I gave up the hunt and went ahead with getting Beverly ready for bed. I wheeled her into the bathroom, picked her up and sat her on the stool. Then I reached down and lifted her bulky net sweater off over her head. When I did this, I heard "plink." Sure enough, when she pulled the ring off, it caught on the loose netting of her sweater.

Beverly's arms could no longer be depended on to move as her brain instructed them. She could not lift a glass of water to her lips. It was just as apt to be flung across the table as to reach its intended destination. Her nerves were losing their insulation and becoming as useless as a bundle of electrical wiring that had all its insulation removed and then had voltage applied.

I had worked for the same company for thirty-eight years starting as a day laborer, moving to assignment man in Production Control, becoming Supervisor, and last being over all of the operations in production. The factory had changed and so had my responsibilities. I was responsible for Factory Administration, Production Control, Processing Engineering, and tooling. The company started out as Bendix. Then it was purchased by Allied, and Allied became Allied Signal. It was a very large, self-insured company. That meant if you were valuable to them, the company would provide any benefit you needed that would allow you to continue being useful to them. At that time in my life all I had to do was ask. I found out later how quickly that benefit could disappear. Even so, while my company was paying those large bills for me, there was a feeling deep inside of indebtedness to them. Well, that isn't exactly true. I am a Christian. With my Lord's help and strength, I did what was necessary to fulfill my responsibilities to my family and my employer, and I appreciated every favor my company granted me.

We found the help we needed in a home health care organization. Allied Signal covered all expenses with no paperwork involved for me. In three years, I never once saw a bill or a receipt of any kind. When I had to work late or Saturday, all I had to do was call, and help would be there to take care of Beverly. Cheryl's care was a different story.

Any time I wanted to get away, either on company business or personal time, it was a must for me to cover the arrangement, and the cost to cover anything other than Beverly's personal care. That usually came from either our daughter-in-law Sherry, or Bev's sister Margie.

Margie was a dear friend to me. We could banter back and forth in good-natured fun. When Margie was not tied up with her own family problems, she would come out to our home each Monday afternoon and cook for us. This also gave her opportunity to visit with Beverly. I would usually get home around four, and Cheryl's bus would deliver her about five. When I entered the house Margie, would be sitting on the couch near Bev's chair reading the paper. I would ask, "Are you fixing supper for us?" Her response would always be, (as she looked at me over the paper), "Yep, why, what time did you want it?" "Oh, five would be nice," I would answer. "It'll be ready," Margie would say, never taking her eyes off the paper.

How the Monday evening meals came together in an hour's time was beyond my ability to understand, but they did, and it happened week after week. They were good: mashed potatoes, a meat dish, and a vegetable, all without fail. It was a treat.

Even with all the favors and treats her Aunt Margie supplied, Cheryl never warmed up to her. One evening there was a family gathering at Jan and Gino's home. (By this time, all five of Margie's children had married and some had children of their own.) The girls and Gino were playing a game with Cheryl. If Cheryl was ever in love with any one, it would be Gino. Anytime she could sit next to him, she did. That is where she was as they played the game. Gino would point to each of her cousins in turn and ask Cheryl; "Cheryl do you love Jan?" Cheryl would rest her chin on her hand, and after a second or two she would nod her head. The question was asked about each person in the room, and the response was the same until they asked her if she loved Aunt Margie. This time her hesitation was a bit longer, and with a peevish grin on her face she shook her head no! They all knew what she would do, and to everyone's delight that was her answer. All of Margie's kids laughed. I know it sounds cruel, but it did not bother Margie in the least. There were many times when we visited Margie in her condo, and Cheryl would refuse to get out of the car. I'm sorry to say she felt the same way about her sister-in-law Sherry.

All of the people I enlisted to help, except Margie were reimbursed. There were others who asked to help out, and I sometimes accepted their generosity. Those were also without pay.

Our son Tim's wife Sherry was a monumental help all during Bev's illness. Later on when things came apart for Cheryl, Sherry was the person who bailed me out the most often. Even though I paid Sherry well and helped them in other ways, when Cheryl's life was over, everything was not as it had seemed to be.

The people that were provided by the home health care organization all did their job. Some worked by the book while others did much more than the rules called for. When I think of a person who went far beyond the call of duty, I think of Clesta Turner. Even though Clesta worked for the same company as the other visiting nurses, she became a wonderful friend. She did washing and even ironed my shirts, but she did much more than that.

No two days are the same when caring for a late-stage Multiple Sclerosis patient. One time a medication will cause a bowel movement; the next day it will not cause any measure of success. Beverly was being lifted and moved each day using a barrier free lift, complemented by a sling. If great care was not exercised in installing the sling, skin could be broken or removed, leaving bare flesh. Difficult is not a strong enough word to describe the effort required to heal such a sore. It sometimes took weeks of applying medication and using sterile pads.

Clesta helped me out of a very real trauma more than once. In one such incident, I had given Bev a suppository in the hope she would have a bowel movement. Instead her bowels just seeped excrement all night long. By the next morning, the problem was still present. Clesta came as I was leaving for work. I told her what was going on and left. It dominated my thoughts throughout the day, and when I came home

Clesta was working with Bev, cleaning her up. I asked about the bowel problem. Without turning around, Clesta said, "I took care of it."

"How?" I asked.

"Beverly was impacted, I dug it out with my fingers," Clesta responded. "Mister Grant, sometimes you just do what you have to do." With that, nothing more was said. Clesta finished up and left. She had not turned toward me or looked my way when she spoke. It was apparent she had had a very traumatic day and was glad for it to be over. I got Clesta's message, and I had the information I needed to take care of Beverly's bowel problems if they would not work on their own, which from then on they rarely did. It may sound like an awful thing to have to do, but it was not to me after I realized its necessity. These were the kind of times that had to be faced often in the last three years of Beverly's life, times when I would recite my marriage vows, "Care for, love, until…"

Chapter #9

Retirement — Not Really

In the fall of 1993 my good friend Charles Parker, a supervisor at work, turned in his paper work declaring his intent to retire. "Charlie" was the person who looked after my responsibilities when I was absent. I did the same for him when he was off work. We had a great working relationship. I also planned to retire and leave at the end of the year. We both knew we were putting our good friend and manager in a hard spot, but each of us had extenuating circumstances we were dealing with.

Even though I had help at home when I was at work, the evening would go along fine; however, in the late hours of the night, I would find myself taking care of my wife's needs. I had to get myself ready for work, get Cheryl up and dressed, give her breakfast and have a lunch ready for her to take with her when she left for work. To accomplish all this by 6:30 and have Cheryl ready when her driver arrived was becoming a too much to handle.. I needed to be up and moving before 5:00 AM.

I turned in my papers and called Social Security to announce my plans. As soon as the Personnel Department heard of my plans, I received a mailing from our insurance company informing me that home health care was no longer covered by my policy. They had covered us for the past three years, but as of November 1st, the company would no longer pay.

I did not immediately understand what was going on. I complained. I made phone calls. I wrote pages of words explaining how there must be some mistake. Then, it dawned on me. The company had been covering me because they needed me, but now that I had decided to retire, that help from them was gone.

I still needed to fulfill my obligation until the end of the year for my work place and my family. I got busy and lined up people to fulfill the need of Bev's personal care while I was at work. I already had a person coming in to clean house for us. All this was expensive, but I had no choice.

Things were working. Everything was getting done. The Thanksgiving holiday was on the horizon. I always looked forward to Thanksgiving. It had been a habit for many years to go to Missouri to spend this holiday with my family. Both of my brothers treated this as a very special time, and they always made the necessary sacrifices to assure that it remained our yearly reunion.

On November 3, 1993, I received a telephone call from my half brother Bill. Bill was planning a trip east. His desire was to visit friends and family, and he was hoping I could help him accomplish his plans. My reward would be to have him spend some time with our family. I did help him. It was a treat for us. At the appointed time I picked him up at the airport in South Bend, Indiana. That evening he was able to see my son Tim, his wife Sherry, and their two sons Jonathan and Tyler. The next morning he borrowed our car to drive to Ohio to visit friends there. The following day he planned to take a bus to visit the family in Missouri.

My mother needed a new TV and entertainment center. I had already purchased these items but until then had had no way to get them to Missouri. I told Bill about my need to get the TV to mom and made a deal with him. He would give me the money that his bus trip to Missouri would have cost, and I would fly him to Willow Springs. Fortunately, the flying club's *Cessna Skyhawk* was available, and I had vacation days left. I found people to take care of Bev and Cheryl, and I was ready to go. Well, I was ready, but the weather would give us a very hard time.

We were at the plane by 8:30 and had already strained, stretched, and shrunk our cargo until it was stowed aboard the small aircraft. We had filed an Instrument flight plan to Willow Springs, Missouri, with a refueling stop in Decatur, Illinois. We had a solid cloud layer at five thousand feet with icing conditions in the clouds. Everything was as forecast. The plane gathered ice going up as we left South Bend, and it iced up when we went down for fuel at Decatur. We had a thirty-knot headwind all the way to Missouri and didn't land at Willow Springs until 1:30 in the afternoon. Actually, our destination on our instrument flight plan was Mountain View, Missouri, because Willow Springs had no instrument landing procedure. When we were given the ADF landing procedure at Mountain View and were safely below the cloud layer, I asked Kansas City Center to cancel our flight plan. Then we turned northwest, flew the thirteen miles to Willow Springs and landed.

My brother Bill went directly from the plane to the pilots' shed to plug in his breathing machine. Bill only had thirty percent use of his lungs because of his many years of smoking. I had not noticed him having problems during the flight, but then he never complained about anything. While he was catching his breath, I was able to get help from the locals to fuel the plane. My brother Don came to the airport with his Cadillac ambulance, which he normally used for hauling mom and her wheelchair around. We loaded the TV into Don's vehicle, and he drove us the quarter mile to mom's home.

November 6th was my mother's birthday, and this was the 5th, so her birthday present was only a little early. My visit with mom was very short. I was on the ground less than two hours before I had to return to the airport to get ready for take-off. I had used Mom's phone to pick up the instrument clearance that would allow me to fly home in the deteriorating weather. I said my good-byes, boarded the plane, arranged my charts and started the engine. Bill walked out in front of the plane and gave me a military salute. I didn't think much about it at the time, but it has come back as a haunting memory many times since. I had no idea it would be the last time I would see my brother Bill alive.

I had filed to fly at seven thousand feet, but when I reached that altitude it was not high enough to remain clear of clouds, so I obtained clearance to go to nine thousand feet where I found the sunshine and warmth needed to clear the ice the plane had picked up during the climb.

Daylight was gone by the time I reached St. Louis. The only stars I could see were moving. They were other aircraft, not stars. There was no moonlight at all.

I did not look forward to the prospect of executing an Instrument approach at Decatur, Illinois at night under icing conditions. In the twenty plus years of flying in and out of that place, never once did they let me use the ILS range. They always pushed me off to the least precise system, the VOR approach. Sure enough, that was what I received when I signed in with them. Another thing I disliked about the place was that they did not like it if you requested a change in the instructions they issued. Well, guess what? That is what I had planned to do. When they gave me the VOR approach, they also told me to descend to five thousand feet. My response to that was: "Please allow me to stay at my present altitude until I am inbound on the approach course." It was allowed, and I ignored the hatefulness of the tone of voice. Spending the additional time at five thousand feet would have caused the plane to take on a heavy load of ice, which could have been hazardous. As it was, with the time it took to refuel, refresh myself, and get a bite to eat, the ice was gone or loose enough to be removed from the leading edges of the wings by scraping it with a comb.

It is hard to believe what people will do when they feel they must be somewhere by a certain time. It may be foolhardy, even dangerous. It doesn't matter. They just want to get there. All day I had been fully aware that I needed to return home that night. As I sat at the run-up area of the active runway in Decatur, Illinois, I couldn't get the instrument lights to turn on. I was about to give up on the needed lights and go on just using my flashlight to see the gages. Fortunately, I discovered the rheostat switch right next to the ignition switch. I flipped it, and the lights came on. God does come to our rescue when we need Him.

I told the tower I was ready for take-off and was on my way. As I was climbing to my assigned nine thousand feet, the plane began to shake, the instrument dash literally jumped up and down! I realized that the propeller had gathered ice. Ice had come off one half, but not the other. I keyed the mike and declared an emergency. As the controller was giving me instructions to return to the field, the ice came off the other end of the propeller, and the aircraft smoothed out. I requested permission to continue on with the filed flight plan, and it was granted. The next problem occurred when I reached nine thousand feet. I was still in the clouds, and still gathering ice. I asked for eleven thousand feet, and they gave it to me. I had to fudge another two hundred feet to stay totally clear of the humps in the clouds and the dreaded ice. When Decatur approach turned me over to Chicago Center, I could hear them stacking incoming traffic into holding patterns as far south as the Knox VOR twenty-five miles southwest of South Bend, Indiana. I was greatly relieved when I crossed over the Knox VOR and was handed off to South Bend approach. South Bend told me to expect the ILS 27 approach. I requested permission to remain at my present altitude until he turned me inbound on approach. The controller granted the request and added that he understood my concern for the ice I would gather when I did descend to the approach altitude of twenty four hundred feet. I did not do well on the approach. I flew through the localizer beam twice before I finally got it right and hooked up. The needles came into play. I turned into the runway heading, and there was the "Bunny Rabbit" hopping right down the approach path. It was a beautiful sight, but the hazards were not over. I was carrying a load of ice, and I needed to keep the speed up with plenty of power on. This runway was not into the wind. When the plane did touch down, it started to nose over because of my speed and the wind coming from behind. I gave the plane a burst of power to force the tail down and let it settle onto the runway. I was thankful to be home. I thanked the Lord God and promised Him I would care for Cheryl and Beverly with all that is within me and gladly do so. Oh yes, I also kissed the ground when I got out of that plane.

Three weeks later we drove back to Missouri to celebrate Thanksgiving with all the family gathered there. Beverly was still feeling well enough to enjoy the trip and the people. Cheryl always took great pleasure in a long ride in the car. She liked to add her input into where we would eat. Also, I think she enjoyed the closeness the ride provided.

Chapter #10
Farewell Bill

December 1993 brought to a close my employment with the Allied Signal Corporation. By the end of that month, I would have been with them forty-three years and four months. However, things did not go as planned. On December 20th I got a call that my brother Bill had passed away during the night. Because of the Christmas holiday, December 23rd was to be my last day at work. With my brother Bill's passing, the 20th would be my last day. I didn't miss the celebration or parties. I did not feel like celebrating anything. My mind was in a whirl. I really needed to do many things quickly.

My younger brother Al lived in Denver. I called him, and we agreed to meet the next day at Bill and his wife's home in Grants Pass, Oregon. I called to see if any of the family in Missouri was planning to make the trip. Nobody was. I then busied myself setting up people to care for Beverly and Cheryl and breaking the news to my boss at work that I was essentially done, retired. Ralph Link was a great person in my book. The last thing I wished to do was hurt him or make things hard for him. Being the understanding person that he was, he knew what I needed to do, and he gave his blessing and extended his sympathy. He did, however, strongly suggest that I come back after the first of the year so the people who worked for me and with me could bid me farewell, and I agreed to do that.

My brother William David Grant, at seventy-two had led a full, active, service-filled life. After serving in Europe in World War Two, he remained in the active reserves and was called into service in the

Korean conflict. He retired from the Los Angeles police department after twenty-three years of service because he was injured in a police car accident while on duty. He also retired from guard duty at the Los Angeles International Airport. He had purchased a burial site at Forest Lawn Cemetery, but his wife Millie gave that to the Grants Pass undertaker for a lot in a local cemetery.

Al and I went to the funeral home that handled our brother's body to find out how things would be done. We asked if there would be a viewing. No, because no one would come. We requested one be held anyway, and it was. Sure enough, only one person came. We couldn't believe it. It was hard to see such a useful life end so quickly.

For me to go back to work to tell my fellow workers goodbye was a bittersweet experience. They gave me gifts. They gave me money, and we made promises to keep in touch. I guess everyone does that, but that is not the way it has gone. We just move on to whatever comes next. Anyway, that is what I did.

My retirement just let me change jobs. First, I rid myself of the cost of a cleaning person and the people who were providing Beverly's care. I wanted to do it all, and I did. I enjoyed the house cleaning, getting the meals, and caring for Bev. Cheryl's care was old hat. For the past three years, I had made sure she was dressed and fed in the morning and ready to walk out the door with her full lunch bucket to meet the bus at 6:30.

Beverly's care was ever changing. One day her bladder would discharge fluid all day. Another day her bowels would not move. She would choke on a food item that had not been a problem before. Flexibility was a must. She was easy to work with, but occasionally she would rebel. For example, she would decide she no longer wished to take her food supplements. For many years, Beverly had been a Shaklee vitamin representative. She not only purchased for herself but for others as well. Now all her food supplements and vitamins had to be ground into powder. When I was still working, I had a machinist make a pestle out of stainless steel. The thing must have weighed two pounds. Using that and a bowl made short work of grinding up the pills. Grinding the pills did not change how they tasted, and that was a problem. I fed her the pills a spoonful at a time, but she could taste them. To help her, I mixed them into something that tasted good. Then, all of it tasted like pills!

Beverly's changes, at least, were understandable considering the chronic disease that was ravaging her body. But I did not understand what was happening with Cheryl about the same time. She had stopped putting a pad on when her monthly period started. She no longer cleaned herself following a bowel movement. She would change panties until she solved the problem. Bev and I had done our best to make life for her as near normal as possible. Bev had worked with Cheryl until she could put a pad on as well as Bev could. She worked just as hard at getting Cheryl to clean herself. We were careful to keep all the necessary supplies available and in the same place. Eventually what was happening would become clear. For the present, though, it was a mystery.

Chapter #11
A BAD YEAR

The year 1995 was an infamous year for our family. Our daughter-in-law's father died of colon cancer. My sister-in-law Millie, Bill's wife, died of cancer. My younger brother Al's wife Jeanine died of lung cancer.

Sherry's father was a pastor and had only been retired for a year or so at age 66. He and I were good friends. In his retirement, he was a great help as a handyman for my son Tim and his wife Sherry. He loved to fish, and he had purchased a home on a small lake about halfway between their two daughters' families. I went to see him during his final days and read to him Ruth 2:12 "May the Lord repay you for what you have done. May you be richly rewarded by the Lord, the God of Israel, under whose wings you have come to take trust." When I finished reading, he was still for a moment. Then he said, "That would be good." A few days later he was gone.

My sister-in-law Millie had been diagnosed with Melanoma several years ago when a small growth appeared unexpectedly. It was removed, and Bev and I took Tim, Sherry, and their two sons, Jonathan and Tyler to visit them in Grants Pass, Oregon. My thinking was that unless we did that, the boys would never get to meet their Aunt Millie. Seemingly, nothing came of the Melanoma. However, when Al and I were with Millie at the time of her husband Bill's funeral, I remember her complaining about severe pain in her back. A little over a year later, cancer took her away. I flew out to Oregon to attend Millie's funeral and gather Bill's personal effects. What remained of my brother's personal effects was stuffed into two suitcases, and I brought them home to be divided between my two remaining brothers and me.

Jeanine lived fourteen months after being told she had fully formed lung cancer. She and Al refused what was then the standard Chemo line of treatment and went off to Mexico to seek other forms of medication. She tried everything except Chemo. She was sure she could beat it, but the cancer took her at Christmas time. Beverly's MS had progressed to the point that it was unthinkable for her to fly. So, my son Tim and I left in the afternoon of Christmas day to be with my brother Al and his children. It was an extremely difficult time because Al's family and mine were very close.

Another thing that happened that year reveals a person's propensity to use unwise judgment when confronted with heavy responsibility and stress.

The Missouri family Thanksgiving trip was on as usual. Beverly wanted to go. At no time during her illness did she elect to stay at home if there was a possibility of traveling to enjoy people. Certainly, that was the sum and substance of Thanksgiving at the home place in Missouri with family.

It was to be a one-day trip of six hundred miles from Northern Indiana to South Central Missouri. We were four hundred miles into the trip going through St. Louis when the left side of my chest began to hurt. As we continued, the pain moved up to my shoulder area and settled there. My niece Donna, a practical nurse thought it was gallstones. I was able to manage the pain well enough to get through Thanksgiving day. However, after I had put Beverly and Cheryl to bed, I tried to lie down but could not. The pain was worse lying down. I toughed it out until about two thirty in the morning. Then I got Bev and Cheryl up and dressed, loaded the car, and we headed for home. I did not even want to think of having surgery in this part of the country. The evident prejudice was brought about because in 1948 I had an appendectomy in West Plains, Missouri, and I still carry the ugly five-inch scar in the middle of my abdomen. I know much has changed in nearly forty years. For sure the fees have changed. My total bill for the surgeon and a ten-day hospital stay was $250.00. With the help of some pain pills found in my shaving kit, we made it home to Indiana in the usual twelve hours traveling time. Some hours later, I got a call from my Brother Don's wife Hazel in Missouri chewing me out for not calling to let them know we had actually arrived home.

The pain in my upper torso was constant. I spent the next three weeks in and out of the doctor's office and the hospital for lab tests. Near the end of the third week, while Doctor Spaulding was examining me once again, he spotted one lone pimple on my stomach, and he exclaimed; "My *#@ it is SHINGLES". He prescribed medication, and in a few days the pain was mostly gone.

The whole episode had frightened me. I had been losing weight along with everything else. My son Tim had asked my doctor if there was a possibility that his dad would not live as long as his mother. Doctor Spaulding's answer was, "That is a distinct possibility."

My niece Donna, my older brother's daughter, currently living alone in Missouri, had visited her son when he was serving in the army and stationed in Europe. She asked if I would consider inviting her along if I ever decided to fulfill my dream of touring Europe. Even though her son was back in the States by then, she had really enjoyed her visits to the Old Country and looked forward to the possibility of going back.

I had often spoken of touring Europe. Beverly and I both had wanted to do that, but now her bout with Multiple Sclerosis had taken away any chance of that for her. So when Donna brought it up, I began to think of it. Beverly and I had done a lot of traveling, and we had used a travel agency for some of it. I called Edgertons and inquired as to what sort of packages they might have, and they sent me material. This would be the start of one more unwise move.

Since my retirement, I would try to get away from my caregiver job a couple times a year. I was not trying to be a hero by any means, but I did want to take care of myself. Even though I always felt guilty when I was away from the work and responsibility of caring for Bev and Cheryl, in my mind at least I knew it was good for me to do it. The help I enlisted in my absence all got paid, with the exception of Margie, Beverly's only sibling. Margie seemed to enjoy sitting with Beverly and cooking for her and Cheryl. (Even though Cheryl did not like her aunt, she did not turn down any of her cooking.)

Chapter #12
BAD TIMING

As I looked over the travel brochures, I settled on a fourteen-day, ten-country tour. To keep the expense reasonable, I checked double occupancy, separate sleeping arrangement, and inquired of Donna as to whether she was at ease with that or not. She was.

I had spent my life in the church and had held office, and I knew how important it was to protect one's reputation. I had also heard a pastor that I had great respect for say: "The reason people get themselves into trouble is they don't make plans to stay out of trouble." I planned to keep my life clean and protect the reputation of the person I was with. Part of that was accomplished. We did behave ourselves, which wasn't difficult. I was twenty years Donna's senior, and we had great respect for each other. The problem was, there were people who wanted to think the worst and did.

A trip like we were planning takes time to set up and execute. The dates we selected were September 2nd through the 17th. We planned a travel date, as required, before and after the dates of the tour. All that was left to do was get our personal affairs set up so we could carry out our plans when the September date arrived.

As September grew closer my concerns also grew. I would lie beside my wife at night and listen to her breathing while she slept. Beverly's breaths would start slow and normal. Then they would start growing. Each breath would extend, and the next would extend further and then stop! There would be an interminably long gap before the process would restart.

I talked to Doctor Spaulding about what I was witnessing. His reply was direct and startling. "You need to get to your lawyer and have him draw up two papers: First, get a living will. Her will should state what limits Beverly wants taken to maintain her life. Second, get her to give you power of attorney," he said. During that summer we followed the doctor's orders and established that no extreme measures would be taken to maintain Beverly's life. I recall that when we were in the lawyer's office having this done, his secretary who was normally friendly, would not look at me and did not speak to either of us. I felt like a crook at having taken that action.

In the spring of that year, Bev had a choking incident, and I took her to the emergency room. I had removed the object from her throat, but the throat has a memory, and to her, it still felt as if something were there. Anyway, because of that occurrence, Doctor Spaulding ordered a "cookie test" to check on the ability of Beverly's throat to aid swallowing. It was to be done at the neurologist's office. That doctor was a young man, and as he did the usual MS physical, I thought he was going to cry. As he took both of Beverly's hands in his, he said, "There are two or three new medications out there, but we have no idea as yet what affect, if any, they would have in your case. I am so very sorry. I cannot help you."

I found myself going from one extreme to another. Sometimes I would think Bev could live a very long time, and other times at night, I would check to see if she was breathing, and see if she was still alive. It was hard living like that.

The weekend before I was to leave on the trip to Europe, my younger brother Al flew in from Colorado to spend a little time with me and help me celebrate my birthday August 31st. Both of us were more car crazy than was necessary, so on one day we went to the Ray Miller Auto Museum, an antique car museum in Elkhart, Indiana. The next day we drove over to the big car show being held in Auburn, Indiana. There is a museum there located in the old factory building where the Cord, Duesenberg, and Auburn automobiles were once manufactured. It was a great adventure.

The next day was Sunday. I dressed Beverly for church. After church there was a carry-in dinner. As I fed Bev, she ate very well. At this stage of things she could not carry on a conversation, but she could answer a yes or no question. After the social time and dinner, I brought Beverly and Cheryl home and put Bev down for her afternoon nap. Cheryl and I did our usual thing: going through the myriad advertisements that come in the Sunday paper. Around 4:00 P.M. I got Beverly up and asked her if she wished to attend the evening church service. She said she did. The evening went well, and the next morning I kissed her good-bye.

Wise or unwise, September 2, 1996, I started out on the trip of a lifetime for me. I picked Margie up at 7:30 A.M. as she was going to stay with Bev and Cheryl. My son Tim delivered me to the bus station in Mishawaka. That bus deposited me at the O'Hare terminal in Chicago. Donna's flight came in right on time, and I met her at the gate. It was great to see her. I looked forward to traveling with a person I could converse with. Ours was in no way a romantic relationship, but we were very good friends.

We flew to St. Louis where the tour started and from there took an overnight flight to London. We spent two days touring London and the English countryside before we boarded a ship to cross the North Sea to Holland. Our tour covered the usual Holland sites: Amsterdam with its maze of canals, the diamond factory, the cheese tasting, and the windmill. In the evening I called home to see how Beverly was doing. She was doing OK; not good, but OK.

We went on to Germany seeing its cathedral at Cologne, its Red Walled Castle at Heidelberg, the Black Forest and then taking a cruise down the Rhine River. Then we went to Switzerland. On the 8th, a Sunday, we were in Lucerne. As we walked around the city streets, we came to a church that was selling loaves of bread. The bread was loaded with nuts and fruit, and we purchased a loaf. We ate from that thing for the next week.

We journeyed on through the Principality of Liechtenstein and took the long drive through Austria, spending the night in Innsbruck. That evening we opted for the side trip that was offered. We attended a really great musical show. Cow bells, wood blocks, alphorns, and a harp were just a few of the things used to make the delightful music we heard. I tried my best to call home that night, but had no luck getting through.

We continued our travels on south to Venice, and that evening I was able to call home. The news was bad. Bev was in the hospital with a high fever, and her blood count was elevated. A lung x-ray showed the lungs clear. She was feeling better and was taking food. What was I thinking? What was I doing here? What could I tell the tour guide? That my wife was ill? She had been ill for twenty-five years. What could I do if I were there that wasn't being done? There was nothing I could do, so I stayed and decided to try to finish the tour.

We headed south through the lush green hills and valleys of Italy until we reached Rome. Vatican City, the Sistine Chapel with its splendor, and the marvel of St Peter's Basilica were combined with the opportunity to see the Coliseum where so many Christians were killed.

On September 12th in the early morning at 1:00 A.M. the phone rang, it was Tim. He called me to tell me that Beverly was still in the hospital. She had pneumonia, and they had restricted her diet to liquid. He also said she could only remain alive by having a feeding tube installed into her stomach. I reminded him of the living will she had signed that would not allow any extreme measure to be taken to extend her life and that we would need to abide by her will. He said, "Well, that being the case, she is considered terminal, and the doctor has enlisted hospice to help out." He said a hospital bed would be required because she would be coming back home. I told him to go ahead with whatever he felt needed to be done. Years later, he told me he had considered going over my head and allowing the feeding tube to be installed and then rejected the idea.

As I look back on that time, I try to understand my thinking. How did I go on with the tour? Was it because of going through so many bad times in the twenty-five years I lived with Beverly's MS? I don't think I expected her to die. Oh, I don't mean not ever. I mean not then, and certainly not before I could get home at the end of the tour. There had been many times in the latter part of her twenty-five year illness when Bev would be totally without strength, unable to eat or speak.

The tour continued up through Italy, going north to Florence, then to the Italian and French border to the small Principality of Monaco. As we traveled on north through France, we rode on the corporate highways with tollbooths and tunnels every few miles. There was so much to see, and I confess I enjoyed all of it. Donna and I spent a day of sightseeing in Paris. In the evening, our entire group took in a show. We got to our room about 10:30, and I called the desk to check for messages. I had an urgent message to call home.

Tim asked me to come home because, according to hospice, his mom only had a few hours to live. Beverly had no pulse in her arms or legs. Her breathing was shallow, and she was starting to turn blue. He asked what he needed to do. I said, "Please call me back if she passes." He did call at about 12:00 midnight in Paris, 6:00 P.M. in Indiana. I called our tour guide Terry and told him of my problem. He said there was nothing that could be done before morning and that I should meet him at 6:30. Eventually, I did lie down and sleep until 4:00 A.M. I got up, bathed, dressed, and packed. I went to breakfast at 6:00, but I ate very little. I spotted Terry at 6:20. We talked, and he tried to contact the Airport operator, but all he got was a recording with the message, "No calls will be accepted before 7:00A.M." Terry's call after seven got results, and he handed me the phone. The TWA receptionist said they could help me. All I needed to do was get to the airport. Terry said, "I can get you to the airport, but I need your cooperation and that of Ms. Miller. Our bus needs to go to the airport, anyway, to drop off four other people, and I don't want you or Donna to mention the death of your wife. It would destroy the gaiety I am trying to provide for these people." Donna was to continue on the tour, and when I saw her I passed on what Terry had said as I bid her farewell.

When I got to the airport, the TWA personnel were just great. They expedited me right through. It took me a little while to get used to the way the terminal was laid out, but when I understood it, I was soon at my departure gate. I had three hours before my plane was scheduled to board, and I felt a need to put down in writing a tribute to Beverly. That three hours turned out to be a time of grief and praying mixed with tears as I recalled what a great person my wife had been when she had her health.

First, I wrote out Psalm 100, and then I wrote: "A Tribute to Beverly Jean McClane Grant." Beverly was a wonderful wife, mother, and friend, but the most important aspect of her life was her love for her Lord. When she was healthy, she served Him tirelessly with her music. There was never a day too long or a schedule too hurried that she could not find time to help people practice their solos, duets, trios, quartets, choir numbers, or cantatas. She loved people, and she loved the Lord's music. Beverly loved with an intensity that was felt by her children, grandchildren, family, extended family, and church family. For a time that expression has been hindered in great frustration. At last she is with her Lord, free to express herself once again. To God be the glory!

The night before, when Tim had called to tell me that Beverly had passed away, he asked what he should do. I wasn't able to think, and I hung up. After I got myself together, I tried calling him back. It took three tries to be successful. I asked him to use the Warner Funeral Home, Pastor Brian Jones as Pastor of the funeral, Patty Matz Clark on the piano, and Lois Fennimore Leibert on the organ. Lois and Patty are both trophies of Beverly's skill as a teacher and of God's grace. I also asked Tim to line up Gino Desimone, Beverly's nephew, to be the vocal soloist and ask him to sing *"No More Night, No More Day"* and *"Pilgrim On a Journey."* Also somewhere in the program they should use *"Overshadowed,"* the first song I ever heard Beverly play. I really hated myself for being so far away, but I was very thankful that our son Tim was so capable.

The trip from Paris to New York did not seem long. My mind was so full of memories, I did not spend time thinking of travel. I did think of what was ahead. I was in New York, through customs, and on my flight to Chicago in about forty-five minutes. I dreaded the bus ride from O'Hare to Mishawaka, but that was the way the trip was laid out. There was stop after stop and more stops before finally, at 10:15 in the late evening, I arrived at the bus station. I called Tim, and he came for me. I greeted my son warmly, and we headed home. It seemed to me that he was doing very well with the loss of his mother.

When we arrived home and walked into the house, I looked around. When I saw Bev's empty chair, I lost it. I could not control my emotions.

Tim, Sherry, and my grandsons Jonathan and Tyler all gathered around me, and we held one another until the feeling passed. Everything was so bleak and empty without my wife's presence. Together we relived the past few days. The emotions and feelings came out as we went over Bev's last few days. It was 2:00 in the morning before we could bring enough closure to allow us to retire.

On the tour bus, seated one row ahead of Donna and me, had sat a very friendly couple. We had visited with them often. The lady had a bad cold, and the cough that goes with it. On the flight home from Europe I began to get a sore throat, and as the day and night wore on, it became increasingly worse. Even with medication it hurt and made sleep difficult, but I did get to sleep. I even slept through the alarm. Cheryl awakened me at 6:30A.M. I was still able to get her ready to catch her bus since no one had canceled her ride. Cheryl did not act to me like she considered anything had changed. It was the same when her grandfather died. She dearly loved him, and he loved her, but I could not see any reaction from her. I just don't think she could comprehend death.

Beverly passed away on Monday September 16th. I flew home from France on Tuesday. Wednesday would be a very busy day. Some of the things I had asked Tim to do had not worked out, so the day following my return all of it needed to be finalized.

Tim came by the house and drove me to Riverview Cemetery in my car. I had called the director who was gracious enough to work me in. We picked out two lots and paid for them along with the fee for opening and closing the grave. It was a long drive to and from the cemetery, and I wanted to write down Tim's account of all that had happened while I was away. The only paper available was a brown paper bag, so that was what I wrote on. I filled it up and later transferred it to my journal.

I had an appointment for 1:00 P.M. with the funeral home, but I had to change that to 3:30, and they worked with us to try to cover everything. Tim and I joined forces to pick out a blue casket with light blue interior. On the underside of the lid was a picture of a lane with a church at the end of the lane.

From the funeral home we traveled back to Tim's home and picked up Sherry and the boys. Then we drove to the florist shop to select flowers for display in and on Beverly's casket. I decided on a large spray of roses for the casket lid, while Tim and Sherry settled on a special swag to lie inside the lid. For the boys we chose two rosebuds to be put near her hands. Thinking back on it, nothing was done for Cheryl. It is amazing how often the one who does not complain gets neglected.

Two very special friends of our family, Ruth Linn and Jo Cooke brought us a nice dinner of Swiss steak and everything that goes with it. Through the years those two ladies had helped us by sitting first with Tim and Cheryl, and then with Cheryl alone. It was no surprise that they would be one of the first to help out at a time such as we were facing on that day. Eventually, far more food was brought than we could consume.

My brother Al was due in at 7:45 P.M. Tim, Jonathan and Tyler went to the airport to get him. His plane was an hour late, so by the time we visited and people got around to leaving, we were very late getting to bed again.

Thursday was viewing day and the family needed to be at the funeral home at 1:30 P.M. The funeral director wanted us to review everything before any visitors came. People would be starting to arrive at 2:00. We had also brought a good selection of pictures to be put on display that would allow people to see how Bev looked in her healthy years. The funeral home personnel had done a good job in preparing Bev for viewing, but twenty-five years of Multiple Sclerosis had reduced her to seventy-five pounds as it took her life from her little by little.

Visitors started coming early, and kept coming for two and a half hours. My sore throat changed from a sore throat into a very bad cold which promised to make that day and the next even more difficult. The family and I went home to get something to eat, rest, and be back at the funeral home before 7:00 P.M. for the evening viewing. That viewing lasted another two and a half hours. The viewing line extended all the way out the door for the entire time. There were Bev's many friends, former piano students, family from both her mother's side and her father's family. There were people from my work and church and former caregivers. It seemed endless. Everyone who knew her well loved

Beverly, and they were very gracious in their comments. I stood by the casket in a daze, partly because of my cold but also because of all that was happening and being said. Still I tried to comprehend all that was said, how it was expressed, and the importance of all those people being present to give the message that Beverly was loved and respected.

Cheryl, Al and I headed home about 10:00 P.M. to get ready for the funeral the next day.

Friday Al and I were still eating breakfast when we noticed it was 9:00 A.M. We were scheduled to be at the church by 9:30 since the funeral would start at 10:00. We made it.

Cheryl had been at the viewing, and she had seen her mother. She was home when her mother was taken away. Sherry had her come up to the casket and say good-bye, but none of this brought emotion from Cheryl. I wish I understood why, but I do not understand. If Cheryl saw me cry, she too would cry. That crying, though, appeared to be sympathy for me, not for what I was crying about. I want to question Cheryl about that when we meet in Heaven and I see her whole and normal.

Pastor Bryan Jones had been our Pastor for eighteen years, but he was no longer with us. He had had two pastorates since he resigned from Twin Branch Bible Church several years before Bev's death. I wanted him to preach Beverly's funeral in the worst way, but it was not to be. A very important person in his current church had passed away on the same day Beverly did, and Pastor Jones was badly needed in his own church. Therefore, we had to settle for the current pastor at Twin Branch.

Beverly's casket was open in the foyer of the church when we arrived. I approached the casket, removed my wedding ring, and put it in Beverly's hand, closing her fingers over it. Then I told her good-bye. I called Cheryl over, and said to her, "This is the last time you will see your Mom." She looked at her mom, and that was the end of it for her. She turned and walked away.

The funeral went well. Lois Leibert played the organ, Patty Clark played the piano, and Gino sang the songs I had requested. He sang beautifully as usual. The pastor told the story of Beverly's life. Others spoke on her behalf including Al. The Pastor used Bev's Bible, and made reference to notes she had written.

Not everything about the funeral was to the family's liking. The funeral director, Mr. Warner, spoke very loudly when he gave his orders to our family in the presence of the congregation and when he summoned the pallbearers. Every time he spoke, his voice grated on our nerves. Even the long trip to the cemetery, where grieving could take place, was not a pleasant time. He did finish his job, and Beverly was laid to rest under some very large trees in Riverview cemetery. Other family members, including her mother and father, are interred in that same area, It is a beautiful area to have as a final resting place, even for a lady who never really cared for the out of doors.

During the funeral service Donna came and sat next to me. She also joined the family for the trip to the cemetery. I was able to visit with her a little during the funeral dinner later. She then introduced me to a new friend. He lived near her in Missouri, and he had driven with her from Missouri to attend Bev's funeral. Donna had become acquainted with David Viers shortly before our European trip, and she had called and talked with him several times during that trip.

Most of the family and a few friends came back to the house for the afternoon and evening. It was good to have the house full.

Al flew out on Saturday. All the company had left. Cheryl and I were alone--so very much alone. Now that Bev was gone, my mind was free to think of her when she was in good health. I missed her. I thought my heart would break it hurt so much. The mailbox was full of cards every day, and people called offering help and encouragement. What a hard time.

I sent a twenty-page letter to my mom to tell her of the trip and what had happened to Beverly. I also sent her a handout from the funeral. Mom was ninety-one and wheelchair bound, but her mind was sharp. She would expect me to let her know how I was doing with it all.

There were lots of things that needed to be done: deal with banks, insurance, investments, pension, and the employee retirement center. There were also things to be returned. A few days later Margie came to help me with thank you notes. She sent notes for floral, monetary, and food gifts. Margie was a real help. She thanked everyone who had shown kindness to our family.

On October 3rd Cheryl and I returned to church. I don't know if it was for her or for me that I had Cheryl sit with me even in Sunday school. Anyway, she didn't seem to mind.

Chapter #13
A Trip to the Ozarks

In mid-October I received a call from Tim. He let me know that he had heard from David, his cousin in Missouri, and that his grandmother, my mom, was in the hospital. He said she wouldn't eat or drink. I decided this was a good chance for Cheryl and me to get away for a while, see mom, and visit the family there.

Mom was in the Ozark Medical Center in West Plains, Missouri. Mom was failing. She required oxygen to breathe, and special instruction for swallowing. She had fluid around her heart, too. The nurses told me she had some mental confusion, but I did not see any of that. I had a good visit with her two or three times each of the three days we were there. When we arrived there on Monday, I didn't know if we would have a place to stay or not. It turned out to be a strange arrangement. I was told that my sister-in-law Hazel, Cheryl, and I would be staying in mom's house, and my brother Don would stay across the road by himself in his and Hazel's house. It did not turn out to be a problem, and Hazel and I had some good talks.

After our three-day visit, Cheryl and I headed home. Cheryl had a very different way of letting me know she was hungry and what she wanted to eat. It was near lunchtime, and Cheryl became excited, laughing, and looking at the traffic. I finally woke up to the fact we were passing a Pizza Hut semi-trailer truck. Cheryl started saying "pizza, pizza, pizza." By the time I found a pizza place, having pizza seemed like a very good idea. I think that is called brainwashing, and it works.

Beverly's sister Margie and her family were so very close to our family that we celebrated everything together. Each year after Thanksgiving was out of the way, the next thing on the docket was Cheryl's birthday celebration. It was now very different--one person short. Beverly was gone. We had to remember Cheryl if for no other reason than she loved a party, any party. There were fourteen of us there, and Cheryl loved every moment of it. Beverly's birthday was the fourteenth of December, and Cheryl's was the fifteenth, so there was no way of getting around the memories. Christmas time had always been a really great time for us as a family as well. Church played an important role, as it should. We had enjoyed it all: the music programs, food, friends, and family. With Beverly and all the care she required gone, I had more time to spend on Cheryl. I looked to see what we could do that we had not done before.

Logan Center, Cheryl's sheltered workshop, needed help for their annual Christmas party. I decided that was a good job for me. I needed companionship, so I would go in search of it. Through the years I had held as many as five different positions at church. I had my regular job as well as the responsibilities of keeping things going around the home and meeting needs of the family. As Bev's illness progressed and required more of my time, I began to shed some of those jobs. With Beverly gone I saw the need to make some changes.

As I worked with different people at the Christmas party, I learned some interesting things about Group Homes. These were houses where five or six mentally challenged individuals lived with one or two caregivers. The premise was to give the clients a better life style. I had never before considered this for Cheryl, but things were developing in my life where this possibility might serve both Cheryl and me. I met parents of individuals much like Cheryl who were both in good health; yet they had moved their child into a sheltered group home. I wouldn't even have thought of such a thing if Cheryl's mother were living and healthy. I had spent three, or the better part of four years bathing Cheryl and Beverly. I could do it without any regard for their being females. I forced myself to totally ignore that part of their being. It was just a job that needed doing, and I did it, but I did not want to spend the rest of my life living that way.

I knew that I did not want to stay single, and I had met a person who indicated she was tired of being alone. She was widowed, and had been for six years. However, she did not want to live in Mishawaka, Indiana, a hundred miles from her grandchildren. Also, she felt living with Cheryl would put an undo strain on a new marriage. That left me with some hard decisions to make. The question was: what will that do to Cheryl?

By the time February rolled around, I started looking into the possibility of securing a place for Cheryl in a group home. It would be a long, drawn out affair. My caseworker was Carol Smith, and she was very helpful but not optimistic. The best I could hope for would be three months for placement.

I felt guilty for thinking of putting Cheryl in a group home and guilty for even dating a woman, but I went ahead with the process. I made application and the process went on its way. Cheryl would need a physical, blood work, Electrocardiogram, the works. If Cheryl passed all that, then a search would be made for a temporary placement for three months.

My journal reads: On March 12, 1997 Cheryl's Aunt Margie and I went to see Carol Smith, Cheryl's case manager. Ms Smith had Cheryl's medical record. Cheryl had passed all the medical exams. We all sat down and discussed what would happen and in what sequence. First, the papers would be submitted, and processing would take four to six weeks. We could not assume that she would be accepted. That was not the way things went at all. Just a few days later Cheryl Davis of ADEC compound in Bristol, Indiana called to tell me they had an opening, and Cheryl and I could come for a visit.

That first visit to ADEC went very well. I was impressed with the home and the personnel. At that meeting, another meeting was set up. We were to come at 3:00 in the afternoon on Sunday March 16th, and Cheryl would stay until 4:30 in the afternoon on Tuesday March 18th. That visit went well also, and they said Cheryl would be accepted. Cheryl liked the place and had made friends with Nancy, a lady with Down Syndrome. There were six ladies in the home they ranged in age from 47 to 73. Cheryl was 42. They said Cheryl had done some hitting, which is out of character for her; however, if you were playing with her, and there was hitting or pushing involved, she did not know when to stop. She would keep going until she got the best of you, laughing the whole time. It was just a matter of getting to know her.

Through the time I had been trying to get Cheryl placed in a home, I had continued to see my new friend, and we had spoken of marriage. Going ahead with all of this meant the sale of my home. When my son and his family learned what was going on, it caused a rift in the relationship between my son and me, but that is part of another story.

It was early April before Cheryl was actually placed into the group home. To make it seem more like her home, her own furniture was moved along with her. Her bed, her triple dresser, the pictures from her room, and the hanging stuffed bears from her bedroom walls all accompanied her. The move for me was very stressful. She was happy as could be. She loved every moment of it.

At the time Cheryl became part of the ADEC compound in April, 1997 it was the ideal set-up. Within walking distance of all the group homes in the complex there, ADEC had their own sheltered workshop. During Cheryl's stay there, I could visit during working hours and see what her assigned job was. I recall on one such visit, Cheryl was placing instruction booklets into plastic envelopes. It was great seeing her using her reasoning process as she tried different ways to get the task accomplished. The plastic envelopes were only large enough for the booklets, with no room to spare. It was a real encouragement to me, seeing her reasoning out ways to make it work.

My personal struggles at this time were mountainous. Too many things were happening at once. Too many things were different from what had been normal fare for the past ten years. For the past six years when we went out to eat I pushed my wife in a wheel chair while mentally handicapped Cheryl trailed along behind us. Both of those individuals needed help securing their food, and one had to be fed while the other needed close supervision. Suddenly, both of those dearly loved people were gone from my daily life. As if that were not enough to throw off my equilibrium, I had become engaged. The woman lived a hundred miles away. Also, I was making plans with her to move to where she lived and to sell my home in Mishawaka. My mind was a mess. Depression, insecurity, and guilt were my daily companions.

I checked in on Cheryl on a regular basis, and every report showed she was doing just fine. I would call and ask permission to take her to McDonald's for lunch, but her thrill of that experience seemed to be dwindling.

I was married to Bernis L. Deters on May 17, 1997. It had been just eight months since Beverly had passed away. The marriage had occurred far too soon to suit my son and his family, but I could not leave them out of my life; so my son and his family were included in the wedding and the following reception celebration. They rewarded me by making it obvious that our relationship was estranged. I had even asked my son to be my best man. I was going on the love I had for him and the memory of the friendship we had enjoyed all of his adult life. That's how it was until I pursued a relationship with Bernis. We also made a place for Cheryl in the wedding. Cheryl was very good in a crowd, very agreeable and well behaved.

As I look back over my journal of that time, I don't see Cheryl mentioned, even though, I know she was at the wedding. I also know, I relied a lot on my son and his family to help with Cheryl. Maybe I expected too much of them. Everything I did caused the gap between us to widen, though it did not come out in full bloom for several years.

The next few months after my marriage to Bernis I neglected Cheryl. I hope it was because I was building a life with a new family. It is not a new idea I am sure, but when you marry, you get more than a spouse. You get another family as well, and family takes time, time I was willing to give even at the expense of neglecting my own people.

When I moved out of my home in Indiana, I loaned it to a missionary family for a year. Their only expense was to pay for the utilities and the taxes. The missionaries were Gary and Lois Liebert. To say they were good friends seems a gross understatement of facts. They were the best kind of people, people whom God had used on the mission field for many years. They cared as much for our family as I did for theirs. I did not visit them in that home, but the ties to that area were strong. In September after my marriage in May, I took Cheryl back to the Twin Branch Bible Church, where I had attended for over forty years and where everyone knew Cheryl. Cheryl and I both really enjoyed that day. There was a carry-in dinner after church that allowed for more than the usual time for visiting. When the visiting time was over, I returned Cheryl to her group home and then I drove back to Grandville, Michigan, to my home with Bernis.

The next big event with Cheryl was at Thanksgiving time. On the 26th of November, I drove to Bristol, Indiana to pick up Cheryl and sign her out to my care for the holiday weekend. I took her to Osceola, where Cheryl's former hairdresser gave her a perm. Like many other things with Cheryl, getting her hair done was a big deal. She complained all through the washing, the drying, and the curlers. She gave the beautician a hard time every minute of the ordeal even though, the same person had been doing this job for her for several years. The beautician knew how to do it without getting water in her face, and she knew every other trick Cheryl had to make her job difficult. As odd as it may seem, when the perm was combed out, Cheryl would look in the mirror, lift the palm of her hand up to her hair, bounce the curled ends and say, "See, See." While we were close to Mishawaka, I took Cheryl to see her Aunt Margie for a short visit before Cheryl and I headed back to my home in Michigan.

Cheryl's visit to our home in Grandville took a little adjustment. It helped greatly that Cheryl adapted so well socially. That night, a birthday party was planned at my stepdaughter's home in nearby Hudsonville. Denise and her husband Rick had three sons, Coltan five, Baylor three, and Canyon four months old. Cheryl dearly loved babies. Any baby was ok. She was not picky. She made over Canyon, but Baylor was afraid of Cheryl. He called her "him" and named her "Jonah." By the time the evening was over, all three of the boys had warmed up to Cheryl—some. Cheryl's birthday was not until December 15th, but she had been included in the celebration and everyone gave her a present.

We were up early the next day, and drove the 637 miles to my mother's home in Willow Springs, Missouri. We had a good trip, and it was good to have someone to help with Cheryl. Not that she needed a lot of help. Most of what Bernis did had not been done for a long time. She did little things like seeing that Cheryl cleaned herself, washed her hands, etc. Cheryl had her own standard of cleanliness, but usually it wouldn't have met anyone else's standard.

We were in Missouri for six days, counting travel time. There were thirty people at Mom's for Thanksgiving and there was enough food to have fed twice that many. Cheryl enjoyed herself because this was where she had spent every Thanksgiving all her life. There was plenty of time for catching up on the news with my brothers, nephews, and nieces. This was all new to my new wife Bernis. As for me, it was great to be with a person who could take care of herself and even help out in the kitchen.

As we traveled back home, I noticed that Cheryl didn't seem to be as enthused with her surroundings as was her norm. She had always enjoyed traveling. Just to be going somewhere was good enough. Maybe, it was being with Bernis whom she didn't know very well, or it may have been an indication of what was ahead for her. Anyway, we made the trip in one day with a stop in Bristol, Indiana, to drop Cheryl off at her group home. There was no one at the home, so we dropped her off at the men's home in the care of the two ladies who were the caregivers there. When we arrived at our home in Grandville two hours later, I called Cheryl's house to see if she had been taken where she was supposed to be. All was well, and I could rest easy that she was cared for.

As I get older, I regret many things that I allowed to irritate me. We were nearly always short on money, and having Beverly and Cheryl's birthdays come just a week before Christmas always posed a problem for me. It never kept me from spending what needed to be spent to properly celebrate the occasions. Beverly's birthday was the 14th of December and Cheryl's was the15th. So on the anniversary of Beverly's 65th birthday Bernis and I were making plans to celebrate Cheryl's special day. The next day we drove to Indiana to get Cheryl ready for a party. By 5:45 in the evening we were at Cheryl's house. We redressed her. Bernis worked with her hair, and we took her to Pizza Hut. Her brother Tim, sister-in-law Sherry, nephews Jonathan, and Tyler were there. With them were her Aunt Margie and all her children. Cheryl's cousins were all waiting for Cheryl so the celebration could begin. Cheryl enjoyed every moment of it.

On Christmas day, Bernis and I went back to Indiana to celebrate Christmas with Aunt Margie's family. Margie was Beverly's only sibling, and we enjoyed being together. They loved Cheryl, and Cheryl loved them (except for Aunt Margie, as I mentioned before). I was really thankful they accepted my new wife. Cheryl's cousins, Jan, Rachelle, and Bethel all made over Cheryl, and she ate it up. As always, we had a great time.

Chapter #14
Too Many Changes

Through the winter and spring of 1998, I visited Cheryl once or twice a month. She always seemed happy, and her housemates loved her. They may have loved her a little too much, because they would do everything for her. That was not good. Cheryl would not do for herself anything someone else would do for her. Bev and I had spent years teaching Cheryl to do for herself, and all that was going away at a rapid pace. There was a bump in the road in March. It was near the first of March on Monday, that I received word that Cheryl had spent the weekend in the hospital, because of a cut on her eyeball and eyelid. This concerned me greatly. I prayed for her often and my heart ached for her. I knew how she was when she got something in her eye, how she fought with it, and wouldn't leave it alone. No amount of instruction would change her actions. Thankfully our eyes heal quickly, and hers did that time as well.

In April of 1998, the bargain I had struck with Lois and Gary Leibert, for a year's free lodging was up. They were well ahead of me, and they had already found a place to stay. As soon as they moved out, I started fixing little things around the place. The new brick patio needed the most work, but there was painting to be done as well. I would go down for a day or two at a time and work on the place. I needed to enlist the use of a realtor, and I wanted to have a public sale, which would require the use of an auctioneer. I found both in one person. I thought this was fortunate. However, as a realtor the man was ineffective, and as an auctioneer he treated me badly. That is the bad side. The good side was that I got rid of my household items. Most of it was given away or hauled off to the dump thanks to my good friend Norwood Gay who carried it away in his pickup truck.

The sale of the home occurred in a very different manner and with the use of a different realtor. The place had been on the market for about four months, and I was considering lowering the price when my realtor said she and her husband wanted to buy my house. They ended up paying the asking price and the deal was done.

During the summer, when I was in Indiana working on the house and involved in things connected to the property, I visited Cheryl either on my way in or on my way out of town. She always seemed to be doing fine. Since she was in the group home and I was a hundred miles away, we were really out of one another's lives. Oh, I would get calls from the caregivers from time to time. Sometimes, the news would be good, and at other times it wouldn't. One of Cheryl's housemates passed away and Cheryl went to the funeral. I was told Cheryl sang along with "Amazing Grace", and "Jesus Loves me", and the words were clearly understandable. This information pleased me but did not surprise me. There had been times when a perfect stranger would speak to Cheryl, and Cheryl would answer and the word would be as clear as a normal person's speech. The stranger would expect her to continue conversing, but that wouldn't happen. Cheryl might smile or ask for pop or something else, depending on what came to her mind.

In early November 1998, my mother, Cheryl's grandmother, passed away. I felt it would be expected of me to bring Cheryl to Missouri to attend the funeral. That was my wish as well. A fourteen-hour trip was a very tiring experience. I wrote in my journal, "Cheryl is different, or I am different." That was the first sign that a change was taking place with Cheryl, and I did not understand what it was. A month later Cheryl's brother Tim said he could tell Cheryl was digressing. Jan, Cheryl's cousin had told Tim she could see changes as well. This was not good. I was concerned. When we celebrated Cheryl's birthday on December 15, though, she seemed like her old self. All the cousins gathered with her loving on her, giggling, tickling, laughing endlessly, and feasting on one of Cheryl's favorite foods, pizza. Certainly, I felt my concern had been unfounded.

After the sale of my home in Mishawaka, Bernis and I decided to take some of the money from that sale, and purchase a new motor home. We planned to use it to allow us to escape the brutal winters in Michigan by traveling to Florida to stay during the winter months. We spent most of October, November, and December getting set-up for that style of living. We purchased a car we could tow behind our new motor home. By late December we were ready for our winter retreat to the warm South.

I really took advantage of my son Tim and his wife Sherry, for I was relying on them to keep watch on Cheryl. During the first three months of 1999 my journal mentioned communications, once from Tim and once from Sherry, of problems with Cheryl at the group home. Then on March 20th Sherry called to say Cheryl was being taken to see a doctor. That examination determined that Cheryl had a urinary tract infection. Treatment was started, and the following Friday she would have more tests, blood work, and a CT scan. A few days later I called Cheryl Davis, the director of the group home and workshop. Ms Davis said that Cheryl was better from her Infection, but there were other problems. Cheryl needed some adjustment made on her eyeglasses. She needed money for camp and clothes. Ms. Davis said Tim and Sherry told her that they did not have time to meet all Cheryl's needs. Ms Davis continued saying that Cheryl needed a visit from her family, and if we did not have time to come and get Cheryl, she would bring Cheryl to see us. It was becoming clear we needed to be home to take care of Cheryl's needs.

When we arrived back in Michigan and were settled back into normal living, I made a trip to see Cheryl. Cheryl was home, rather than being at the workshop because she had a bad cold. After greeting her, I asked her to get her coat so we could go for a ride. Cheryl promptly did what I asked. The housemother exclaimed, "How did you get her to do that? She won't do anything I ask her to do. "I really didn't have an answer for her except that when Cheryl was at home with the family, she was taught to do whatever we asked of her. I had no explanation for the reason Cheryl wouldn't obey them.

I had some business to attend to in Mishawaka, so I took Cheryl along with me to downtown Mishawaka. I did not notice any difference in her at all. After I had completed my business, we went to visit Aunt Margie, my sister-in-law. Cheryl did not want to go into Margie's condo. Since she had a cold and her aunt was not one of her favorite people, I did not insist. It did not seem strange that she refused to go in. After I finished my visit, I knew Cheryl would be hungry, so we went to the Pizza Hut where we met our good friends Norwood and Genie Gay. Cheryl always enjoyed the Gays. Sometimes she even sat with them in church. We had a really great visit. It was late afternoon when I returned Cheryl to the group home. I felt the afternoon had gone well.

I had planned this to be a two-day visit so I could see my son Tim and his family. After I dropped Cheryl off, I headed back to Mishawaka. Sherry had injured her foot, and that became a part of the conversation, along with the normal catching up on the lives of my grandsons Jonathan and Tyler. We went out for dinner, and when we returned, we looked at some work Tim and Sherry were doing on their patio.

As the evening wore on, nothing was said about my spending the night. I had my coat and hat on before Tim indicated it was OK for me to stay. He said, "Make yourself at home." I said "How much at home? Shall I go get my stuff?" He said "Oh, sorry, sure." This was my first time to spend the night at my son's home.

The next morning, Sunday, I headed back to pick up Cheryl for church. Tim led singing at both the morning and evening services. It was a real joy for me to see him doing what I had done for over forty years and doing it in the same church. Cheryl spent the afternoon with Donnabelle Matz whom Cheryl dearly loved. Donnabelle loved Cheryl, too.

After the evening service we joined the Gronnings, Jan and her girls, Rachelle, Bethel, Tom, and Margie. Cheryl had a wonderful time for two days with some people who had played a major role in her life for many years.

The term "staffing" was used to describe a monthly procedure for apprising a parent of the status of a client employed or housed in an institute such as Cheryl had been a part of for most of her developmental life, and it carried over into group home living as well. I made every effort to be present for those procedures May through December since I had remarried. My wife Bernis and I enjoyed spending the winters where it was warm, but when we were home in Michigan I wanted to do whatever possible to meet the requirements that might be forthcoming from Cheryl's stay at the group home. Keeping her in clothes was a part of those needs. As a result, Bernis and I would take her shopping. Almost all Cheryl's outer clothing needed alteration. This was a job I had done after Bev became too sick to make Cheryl's clothing.

My journals show that I did attend Cheryl's staff meetings. We were faithful on birthdays, Christmas, and other special days or events. The "bumps in the road" caused my conscience to gnaw at me and to question whether I had done everything possible for that special person I had been given.

In August of 1999, Cheryl was taken to Doctor Rae, an eye doctor. Doctor Rae told us Cheryl's eyes were healthy, but her left eye was so severely near sighted that it was not practical to try to correct it. He said it had never been corrected as a child. Because of this the right eye took over and the left eye did not focus. The Doctor said, "The left eye is not blind, it has useful sight for peripheral vision, etc." The doctor would only correct the right eye, and use a clear lens for the left.

I understand the difficulty of an optometrist trying to fit glasses to a child who is non-verbal and cannot understand the questions the doctor asks. Cheryl could not respond to the instructions given because she did not understand what was required of her to enable the doctor to help her. Beverly and I had taken Cheryl to Doctor Andy L. Nemeth of Optometric Associates in South Bend, Indiana. Beverly and I also used him for our eyeglass needs and found him to be a very capable doctor. Beverly had a very difficult prism problem associated with her MS, and doctor Nemeth was able to keep her glasses corrected so she could read almost to the end of her days.

Doctor Nemeth showed Cheryl pictures of comic strip characters and adjusted her glasses based on how she reacted to the pictures. He felt he was doing a good job, and we trusted him. At least he tried. As I recall no other doctor would take her. I am not sure how Doctor Rae could have been so sure of his diagnosis. Once again, we needed to trust the doctor.

Eyeglasses were not the only problem area for Cheryl. Keeping her dental work up to date was a challenge that persisted all her life.

She never became more understanding about someone looking in her mouth, even as she got older. If she needed a filling, the dentist would arrange to have her admitted as an outpatient at the local hospital where she would be anesthetized so he could do his work. With Cheryl and with Beverly in her illness, it was a matter of doing whatever needed doing to keep those two wonderful people moving along through their allotment of life. I was thankful then and am thankful still for the great insurance coverage my employer offered and our God-given good sense to take advantage of it. If I had not, I would still be up to my ears in debt.

In November and December of 1999, I had some troubles of my own. Grace Bible Church in Grandville, Michigan, had organized a short-term mission trip to Slovakia. In one day we flew from Grand Rapids, Michigan, to Atlanta, Georgia, via Cincinnati, and nine more hours to Vienna, Austria. Then we drove to Bratislava, Slovakia, where we boarded an old smoky bus and rode another six hours to a small village where we would work for two weeks.

My job on that trip was to lay tile. This called for me to wear kneepads at least four hours each day. When the two weeks of work were complete, we retraced the same route back home.

We no sooner arrived home than it was time to leave again for Missouri for Thanksgiving with my family. Not many days after we returned home from that trip, I began to have severe pain in my upper left shoulder. I endured the pain for a time, but late one night I asked Bernis to take me to the emergency room. The pain was more than I could stand. Seven hours of tests later, I was diagnosed as having a pulmonary embolism, a blood clot in the left lung. Long travel time and the kneepads had done me in. While I was in the hospital for my problem, Cheryl was admitted to Goshen General Hospital. My journal is unclear as to what was wrong with her. It does say, "Cheryl is back in the hospital. Sherry spent the night with her. Tim was called, and when he got there, Cheryl was doubled over and would not respond. He, Sherry, Jan, and Gino were able to get Cheryl to drink water and other fluids. They all stayed until Cheryl began to respond to them, and she was able to lie down and go to sleep."

I had so many problems I was not able to keep up with Cheryl during that hard time for her. I was very thankful she was near family who loved her and could see that her needs were met.

January 10th was the date Doctor Kobiela gave me as the date it would be all right for me travel again. On the 11th we had our motor home loaded, and by four in the afternoon we were on our way south. I could not leave the area without saying good-bye to my family. The first stop was to see Cheryl at her workshop. Whatever had put her in the hospital, was better, for she was back to work, and according to her supervisor, was doing quite well. However, in the group home they had trouble with Cheryl not doing what she was told. In the workshop no such problem existed. What could be the difference, I wondered? Could it be that in the group home the guidance help was always changing, where in the work area she had the same supervisor every day, and that person became her authority figure? In my mind, at least, that was the answer.

When we arrived in Florida I was by no means a well person. I was running a fever every day. I felt nauseous all the time. We were camped on Sanibel Island just a little south of Fort Myers. I went to see a doctor there on the island, and he sent me to see a well-known pulmonary specialist in Fort Myers. Under his care I was soon feeling fine again. We spent three months there before heading back north.

Our motor home was taking us up I-69 in Indiana when I called my daughter-in-law Sherry. When Sherry answered the phone, she seemed cool toward me. She and Tim had had a hard winter taking care of their family and had been continually called by the personnel at the group home where Cheryl was living. Sherry told me the group home could no longer care for Cheryl's needs, and she and Tim, with the help of Sherry Davis, had found a place for her in Mishawaka, Indiana. Cheryl was heading for a nursing home.

Cheryl had been living in the group home for nearly three years. As I searched through my journals covering the fall of 1999 and the winter of 1999 and 2000, I found very little recorded of Cheryl's troubles that would land her in a constant care facility, so I must go by memory. What a chancy thing that is at my age.

In the fall of 1999, I recall getting a call from one of the caregivers at the group home. She was complaining that Cheryl would not use her fork when she ate. "What!" I said, "You can't be serious." She was serious. I discounted this in my mind. Sure, Cheryl had some unusual ways of eating. She turned her hamburger upside down and tore the bun off a piece at a time before eating what the bun contained. She ate her pizza the same way, starting with the crust. When Cheryl lived at home and we sat down to eat a normal meal, she not only ate with a fork, but she also used a table knife. We occasionally had to tell her to turn her knife over so the cutting edge was against the meat. We had taught her how to cut her meat for a very selfish reason. If we cut her meat for her, she would finish well ahead of us and want ours. It was all part of the weight control thing. Cheryl had an appetite that was healthy and continuous. At the group home there was the obedience problem, and I reasoned: maybe she just doesn't want to do what she is told. I didn't want to believe things were coming apart for her, but they were.

In late fall Cheryl started refusing to get into the bus. This was a real problem for all the ladies in her house and the leadership. If Cheryl wouldn't get in the bus, none of her housemates could go on an outing. I recall being at her house one of the times she was asked to get on the bus. She walked up to the bus and bent over laying her upper torso on the floor of the bus. She would not even try to climb into the seat. Group home living for Cheryl had come to an end.

April 14, 2000, Sherry and I were talking, and she told me she and Tim would be in Bristol, Indiana, at the group home at 3:30 for an afternoon meeting to be held before Cheryl was released. I told her we would be there for the meeting.

When the staff meeting ended, we began the process of moving Cheryl to her new home. We bid farewell to Cheryl's housemates. During the three years Cheryl had lived there, we had gotten well acquainted with her housemates. There were hugs and tears as we said good-bye. We took some of Cheryl's clothes and planned to return the next day to pick-up Cheryl's personal items and furniture. Cheryl's cousins Jan and Bethel met us at the nursing home to help Cheryl get settled in. Jan came back later in the evening to see that Cheryl was ok with her new home. She seemed to be satisfied with her situation.

Bernis and I picked up some pizza and took it to Tim and Sherry's home where we spent the evening visiting with their family. I enjoyed the time very much since I had not seen my family for nearly three months. Bernis and I spent the night in our motor home, and the next morning we had breakfast with Sherry and the boys. Tim came home from work at noon so that we could use his truck to move Cheryl's belongings. The furniture went to Tim's garage to be given to anyone in the family who could put it to good use. Some things were taken to Cheryl's room at the nursing home to make it look more like home to her. Cheryl was not very responsive, so after awhile we left.

It was time for Bernis and me to go home. We filled the car and motor home with gas, hooked the car to the motor home hitch and were soon on our way to Michigan.

Within a week I was back in Mishawaka for the funeral of a dear friend Beverly Gilvin Thornton. It was a sad time, but it was this sort of thing that would provide me with the opportunity to visit Cheryl. I also planned to see Tim and his family. I had not yet learned a very valuable lesson. That lesson is: Children may not feel the same way about their parents, as the parents feel about the children. I was soon to learn that if I expected to visit them, they needed to be informed well in advance. I was glad to see them anytime. That difference would eventually bring disaster to a valued relationship, but on this visit I did not know this. On this visit I saw Cheryl eat her evening meal. She ate all her food, but she looked at me like I was a stranger. When I left Cheryl, I went to Tim's home. We sat around the kitchen table for two hours catching up. I spent the night with them, but I shouldn't have. I did not sleep well, and the time with them in the morning did not go to my satisfaction or to theirs. My welcome was wearing thin, but I was just too stupid to see it.

I went to see Cheryl one more time before heading back to Michigan. Again, she acted as if I were unknown to her. As I sat beside her on the bed, she wet herself. I had no idea what was happening to my daughter, but it wasn't good.

A month later I was back to see Cheryl. I had brought her a TV/Video combination, because she spent so much time in her room. That visit was a refreshing change from the last visit. Cheryl was her normal, happy self.

The first comprehensive evaluation by the nursing home came in June. I had recorded all of their findings: Problems with Cheryl C. Grant; likes to take her shoes and socks off; removes her glasses--doesn't like wearing them; she had one fall; doesn't care to have her vitals checked; doesn't want to be bathed; she eats 95% of her food; she has gained two pounds, she weighs 122 pounds; she has few medical problems, except for wetting herself; she likes music; and her attention span is good observing and watching TV. They had decided to stop her Vita C, and they said, "Cheryl wears Depends at night, but not during the day."

That evaluation casually mentioned two things that eventually would contradict another finding that on the surface seemed like good news. Cheryl's fall and the bedwetting were significant. They were significant because the same report said Cheryl had few health problems. It would be some time before we understood the significance of the fall and her bedwetting as her health continued its downward trek.

When Cheryl really became settled in at the nursing home, she did not spend much time in her room. She was in her element. Cheryl had always paid attention to disabled people. Now she was in a place where everyone had a problem of some sort. She could be seen throughout the day trailing along behind whichever caregiver she had taken a liking to.

Cheryl's first year at Beverly County Side Place was anywhere from good to unbelievable. In the back of my journals, I would write in the date and Cheryl's status. Two months before Cheryl arrived at the nursing facility I wrote: The caregivers tell me, "Cheryl no longer knows what we mean, when we tell her to go to the bathroom. She just goes in her clothes. If she is in bed she goes in the bed. She forgets how to feed herself and has to be fed. She expects everything to be done for her."

In the past eleven months, I had visited Cheryl at least twice a month. On occasion she would be just fine, be in good humor, and seem what I regarded as her normal self. I knew she liked music, so I brought in a "Boom Box." It accepted tapes or CD's. I would play my harmonica for her. Sometimes she liked that, and at other times she would be a real "stinker." She would scream, yell, and would not socialize at all. I had been with her at mealtime and seen her eat all her food unassisted. I never knew what to expect.

The last three years of her mother's life Cheryl was my only companion. It was really hard for me to see her go downhill so fast, but her troubles were just beginning. A month after Cheryl's forty-sixth birthday, she was given a CT scan, and an MRI. With those test results in hand Cheryl was diagnosed with Alzheimer's disease, and Hydrocephalus. She was wheelchair bound, and her bed had been placed on the floor to prevent injury from falling out of bed.

By the time Cheryl's forty-seventh birthday rolled around, it was not a pleasant thing to be in her presence. She would open her mouth, and this awful noise would come out. All of Cheryl's cousins were there, and their love for her would not allow them to be detoured from making over her. The best they could get from her was a half grimace, half smile. Christmas was no better. Cheryl would cry when music was played. Even my harmonica received the same response.

As heartless as it seems in hindsight, Bernis and I left for Florida the end of December, and I passed my responsibility for Cheryl over to Tim and Sherry. I also knew that Aunt Margie and her daughter Jan would be maintaining a watchful eye in Cheryl's direction.

It seemed that "No news is good news." since we received very little input as to how Cheryl was doing through the winter. Even in Cheryl's June staffing, she was regarded as "doing good; eats OK; attention OK; weight 108, down 20 pounds in the past year." In July, Cheryl was in a good mood during my visit. In August, I recorded that she was happy, but she paid no attention to her visitors. The September staffing report went well with nothing of significance mentioned.

When I was at Country Side Place for the early October visit, Cheryl was asleep. I played the harmonica to awaken her. It did wake her up, but she refused to turn over. I nudged her with my elbow as I played. That amused her, but not enough for her to give me the satisfaction of her full attention. Three weeks later, Cheryl would not stir at all. I played for twenty-five minutes, and she would not turn over or do anything to let me know she knew I was there.

November fifteenth, Cheryl was awake and alert. She was responsive, and she sat up, looked at me, smiled and laughed. It was hard for me to know for sure if what I was seeing was Cheryl affirming her independence or if it was illness. I did know that Cheryl could be a real character and often was. That trait in her said, "Just because you want to be my friend, it doesn't make you my friend," or "just because you came for a visit, it doesn't mean I have to entertain your presence." How much of it was my Cheryl being herself?

On December 15th Cheryl had her 48th birthday. We had a party. All her cousins, her aunt, her brother and sister-in-law, and their children were there. Cheryl was totally unresponsive.

The Christmas visit was different. Cheryl seemed to be traumatized about something. This was not good. It really gripped my heart. I was on the verge of tears throughout the visit.

Chapter #15
A Long Ending

Cheryl's status January 2, 2003: Weight down to 90 pounds. She refuses liquids. She will take a little food, but then pushes most of it out with her tongue. She seems to have given up. She will not interact with the staff. The head nurse says Cheryl has six to ten months of life remaining. She will be put under hospice care.

Well, even the end had its ups and downs. In February Cheryl was regarded as stable. In late April, Cheryl's nurse said, "Cheryl is doing fine considering she is a Downs and the late-life problems that accompany that." Her weight remained at 90 pounds. The story would soon change.

The July 15th staffing revealed added challenges for my daughter. Cheryl's weight had dropped to 85 pounds. All the staff was gracious and really seemed to be doing everything possible for Cheryl. Pain was being treated with Tylenol. That meeting was the first time I heard seizure mentioned. They said she was being treated with Tegretol. The meeting continued: Cheryl doesn't eat well and resists anything liquid. I had stopped at Cheryl's Aunt Margie's and asked her to come with me to Cheryl's staffing. When we visited with Cheryl that day she was having a good day.

A call on August 31st from Country Side came with more bad news. They said Cheryl had not eliminated bodily fluids during the past two days. She would not eat or drink, and they were seeking counsel from Cheryl's doctor. When I visited two weeks later there was no mention of a problem. Another two weeks and the downhill track would resume. Cheryl cried during my visit as I played the harmonica for her.

The October 2nd visit went the same way. I felt totally helpless to be a comfort to Cheryl. Any interaction brought tears. I did feel the nursing home was doing everything possible to be as much help to Cheryl as they could.

October 21st dawned cloudy. The weather pretty well matched the day's activity. I headed south to Mishawaka, Indiana. My mind finally was able to encompass the fact that my daughter was going to die. I had better do what I could do to prepare for her final day when it came. My first stop was at Bubb Funeral Chapel. There I meet Frank Gorny. Mister Gorny was an affable person, one who could make this process bearable. He helped me pick out a casket, flowers, head stone, and vault. Then I decided what words would be given to the paper for her obituary notice. He told me what the cost would be. My next stop was to see Cheryl. That day, she let me play my harmonica for her. I hugged her and told her over and over again that I loved her.

It was October 30th when I got the call. The phone call had come when I was not home. It was from Tim. The message was simple. I needed to call him. When I did, I got Sherry. She said, "Cheryl is very bad. You ought to be here." Bernis and I had discussed what we would do when this day was upon us. We did not want to be a burden to my son and his family. We would to take our motor home to Tim's house, park it beside their driveway, and stay as long as we needed to be there.

I had messed up so many times in my life being in the wrong place when I needed to be somewhere else. When Beverly died, I was in Europe. When I had an opportunity to go visit my father in the hospital, I had elected to stay home and take a flight lesson rather than go with my brother Al to visit him. A week later Dad was gone. Al said, "Dad asked, 'Is Lewie with you?'" When Al said, "No," tears came into Dad's eyes.

I went to where the motor home was stored, uncovered the coach, and brought it to our condo. We were loaded and ready to travel about 8:00 p.m. when Bernis's son Dennis came by to wish us well and promised to pray for us.

We arrived at Tim and Sherry's home at 11:00. Having parked, we unhooked the tow car, and drove to the Country Side Nursing Home. Cheryl's appearance was much worse than I had expected: her mouth was open and her unblinking eyes were open. I had not prepared myself for what I was seeing.

Aunt Margie was there as, well as Cheryl's cousins Jan, Rachelle, and Bethel. Tim and Sherry were there also. Everyone stayed until 3:00 a.m., Bernis went back to the coach to get some sleep. Sherry and I stayed until 7:30a.m. At that time I went back to the motor home and showered, ate some cereal, and took an hour-long nap.

Bernis and I returned to Cheryl's bedside between 12 noon and 1:00. Throughout the afternoon different members of the staff came in to see Cheryl, lean down and kiss her, and leave with tears in their eyes. From the time Cheryl went to the nursing home, I had been praying she would have compassionate, loving, people attending to her needs. I felt God had answered my prayers.

As I sat with Cheryl through the afternoon and evening watching the life drain from that dear person, I was reminded of many things about her life. Cheryl could understand more from the tone of a person's voice than the average person could derive from reading the book, **How to Win Friends and Influence People**. I could only guess at all the things Cheryl did understand.

Cheryl drew her last breath at 9:20 p.m. on her very favorite day of the year, Halloween. She had loved the "Trick or Treat" visitors, and thoroughly enjoyed scaring them half to death before dishing out candy to them.

All of the family who were with Cheryl when she passed away went to Tim and Sherry's home and had something to eat. My grandson Jonathan, Tim and Sherry's Son, was away at Asbury College and Tim made arrangements for him to fly home to be with the family.

The next morning started early. A call to Bubb's Funeral Home let them know of Cheryl's death. It also got us an appointment. Tim, Bernis, and I got there by 11:00 a.m., and Frank Gorny reviewed the arrangements with us. He helped us prepare notices for both the South Bend Tribune and The Grand Rapids Press. He walked us through all the details that would cause the funeral service to go smoothly. When

Mr. Gorny was finished with us, Bernis and I headed to the mall to find clothing suitable for Cheryl to wear.

When I asked Pastor Brian Jones to preach Cheryl's funeral, I was very puzzled by his response. He asked, "What is the purpose of having the funeral?" This was such a tender time for me, I thought, "That is not a fair question." But then I did what the question was designed to do. I asked myself, "What is going on here?" Cheryl was no accident. God had given Cheryl to Beverly and me to teach us lots of lessons, and it is too early to stop learning from Cheryl's life. After dwelling on the Pastor's question for a time, I came to the answer: I want this funeral to celebrate Cheryl's life. She was God's gift to our family, our church, our friends, and the lives surrounding our family. That was the answer I passed back to the pastor God had given us for eighteen years. I had prayed with him, led singing for his services, gone with him on house calls, and worked on his car. He knew my family better than I did.

My questions did not end when I gave Pastor Jones the answer to his question. Why, Lord did you give Cheryl to us? That was my cry in the early days. My brother Al reminded me that in the time when Cheryl was expected but not yet delivered, he heard me pray over and over, "Just let this child come into this world healthy and normal." It took me fifteen years of Cheryl's life to be able to thank God for giving her to us. Bringing these thoughts to mind brought me to what should be carved on Cheryl's head stone: "**She was God's gift to our family**."

I knew that God was in the business of building lives. Our happiness and our health was not what life was about. It was and is about what He has to do to reach us with the message He wants our lives to display. Our message on the day of Cheryl's funeral should be the same as our Lord's: "God does all things well all the time, even with Cheryl. She was not defective in His eyes. She was designed for a purpose, and I believe she lived out that purpose. She left this life, but she is with her mother and her Lord, and she is whole, normal, and complete."

Patty Matz Clark had been Cheryl's very best friend, and she was the one playing the organ for Cheryl's funeral. The viewing, the day before, had been packed. The day of the funeral was no different. Why people were so drawn to this person was hard to imagine. It was a very different funeral, for a very different kind of person. Pastor Jones greeted the people, and introduced Cheryl's brother Tim to lead the people in singing "The Wise Man" chorus. Tim also had the people do the motions that go with the chorus that had been Cheryl's favorite. In the evening service at her church, if choruses were being led and requests were taken, Cheryl could be counted on to request "The Wise Man," as she held up two fists, one on top of the other, the sign she knew for building. Tim delighted the guests by telling a story he remembered when he and Cheryl were home as children: He had gotten up during the night to get something to eat, being careful not to wake anyone, especially Cheryl. Just as he thought he had been successful in quietly retrieving a cookie from the cookie jar, he turned, and there was Cheryl, standing, hands folded behind her asking, "Good? Huh? Good?" as she nodded her head and smacked her lips. I had never heard the story, but I know what would have followed. Cheryl would have moved over to where the cookie jar was kept and requested a cookie, by saying, "You?"

Gino Desimone married Cheryl's cousin Jan. When Jan started dating Gino and brought him to church, Cheryl was attracted to Gino. She wanted to sit with them—only she wanted to sit between Jan and Gino, but Jan would have no part of that. When Gino became part of our family, Cheryl took every opportunity to sit next to him. Gino composed a song to be sung for Cheryl's funeral, and with his deep and beautiful voice, he sang it in Cheryl's memory:

Little pigtail girl about thirty-five years old.
Sittin' with her mama on the third or fourth row.
Singing songs about Jesus like "Nothing But The Blood"
Couldn't understand her words but her heart was filled with love.
And those who love her dearly just praise the Lord and say;
"Cheryl Grant's in church today."
I could hear those people saying, "Cheryl Grant's in church today."
And she was singin' her song; "Amazing Grace How Sweet the Sound."
"If a Wise Man Builds His House Upon A Rock It Won't Fall Down."
"When All Get To Heaven What A Day That Will Be."
"There's A Fountain Flowing Deep And Wide With The Father's Love For Me."

The time went on. Her strength was gone. She had nothing more to say.
Sittin' in a wheelchair a million miles away.
In a small room filled with memories of a life filled with love,
Thinking 'bout her home above...
You could see it in her eyes...she was...
Dreamin' 'bout her home above.
And those who loved her dearly just held her hand and prayed
That the God who Cheryl sang to would come and take her home today.
One day Cheryl closed her eyes and went to sleep.
She woke up with the saints of God at Jesus' feet.
She was singing songs so beautiful I could hear the angels say:
"Cheryl Grant's in church today."
I could hear those angels saying, "Cheryl Grant's in church today,"
And she was singing her song; and you know that she sees clearly, like we all will see one day...
Cheryl Grant's in Church today...All my love, Gino November 4, 2003

I do not remember Pastor Jones' words as he spoke to celebrate Cheryl's life. I know I appreciated what he said, and I cherish the time he was our pastor. I never felt that Pastor Jones in any way resented having Cheryl in the service, even though she never warmed up to him. If he offered her a "Hi Five," and she decided to respond to him, she would give him a real "Palm Burner," and giggle as she did it.

I am looking forward to seeing Cheryl in Heaven, I can't wait to ask her when she is a whole person, "OK, Cheryl, what did you really think of our family when we were all together in our home on Terry Lane?"

Epilogue

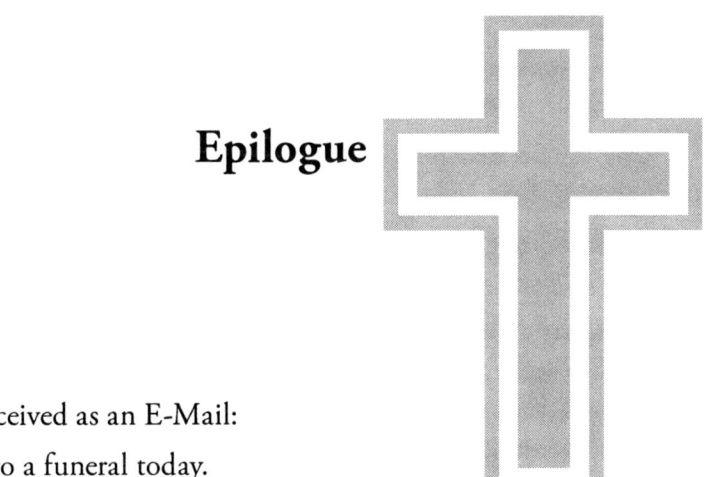

This was received as an E-Mail:

I went to a funeral today.

Occasionally there will be a funeral that makes headlines; generally the person was a celebrity, or Government official, or some other kind of "somebody."

Sometimes you will attend a funeral where the deceased had many contacts and people come to show their respect out of mere obligation.

The lady whose funeral I attended today was not well known. She did not have the distinction of public recognition. She did not have political power. She was not a "somebody."

This lady was 48 and functioned as a two year old. Her life was far from glamorous.

She never learned to read. She could not tie her own shoes. You could not hold a conversation with her. No one sought her opinion.

Today over 150 people came from many miles to share their memories of how Cheryl had impacted their lives. We sang "The Wise Man Built His House upon the Rock," because it was her favorite song. We laughed as we remembered how she turned her pizza upside down before she ate it.

We remembered how she would comfort someone who was crying by patting their shoulder and crying with them. We smiled to think about how loudly she would sing her songs to Jesus, and how proud she was to be allowed to beat a drum during a children's play.

We remembered how she loved babies and would croon, "So Cute!" to them.

Some would say that this woman, who did not ask to be born with Downs Syndrome, had no "quality" of life.

One doctor told her parents to put her in an institution and "get on with your lives."

But another doctor told them to take her home and love her. We all loved Cheryl.

We learned from Cheryl. We learned that sometimes you can get a really big smile from ice cream. We learned that when there are no words to make it all better, it helps to have someone sit and cry with you. We learned gentleness.

Our courts today are embroiled in legal battles over 'quality of life' issues. "Experts" in their fields are assuring us that it is better to end a life that does not measure up to 'their' standard of quality. But they are missing something.

They're missing the blessing that comes from knowing someone like Cheryl, someone who expects little, but gives much, someone who will never know the stress of a nine to five, but who smiles at how Jesus can paint a rainbow. Someone who could not be termed a 'productive citizen,' but who has a childlike wonder at the world God created.

Jesus said that Cheryl was blessed because she was pure in heart; and we know that now she dances in His presence… with a life of such quality as we will not understand until we join her. Perhaps it is our quality of life that needs to be examined.

We were blessed to know Cheryl… and we look forward to dancing with her in heaven.

Author Unknown

LaVergne, TN USA
23 March 2010
176765LV00001B/1/P